FACING YOU, FACING ME

FACING YOU, FACING ME

Race, Class, and Gender
Among U.C. Berkeley Student Leaders

Edited By David Stark and Jerlena D. Griffin

Stiles Hall
Berkeley, California

Library of Congress Cataloging-in-Publication Data
Library of Congress Control Number: 2001088400
ISBN number: 0-9708714-0-6
Stark, David & Griffin, Jerlena, editors

Cover photos (clockwise, upper left): Ana Traylor, Sherilyn Tran, Tel Cary-Sadler, Anthony Kenyon, Hector Coronel, and Daisy Hatch.
Cover Design: Rebecca LeGates
Typesetting: Camha Le
Printer: McNaughton & Gunn, Saline, MI

Please direct book orders and reprinting requests to:

Stiles Hall
2400 Bancroft Way
Berkeley, CA 94704
Telephone: 510.841.6010
Fax: 510.841.0132
Email: info@stileshall.org

Printed in the United States
10 9 8 7 6 5 4 3 2 1

Dedicated to college students everywhere who seek truth
through engagement…
and to Millie whose light shines on.

Special Thanks to: Anika Johnson, Camha Le, Megan Voorhees, Kerri Harper, Luisa Giulianetti, Malcolm Margolin, Genaro Padilla, Harry LeGrande, Bernice Lockhart, John Martin, Betsy Rose, Shirley Griffin, Yossedek Desta, and the Stiles Hall Board of Directors.

CONTENTS

FOREWORD

This seminar grew out of experiences in the seventies and eighties with a voluntary desegregation program, founded by Black inner-city parents and White suburban parents in Metropolitan Boston. That program brought fifty percent Black and fifty percent White high school youth together—there were very few Latinos or Asians around Boston at the time—to work on a common project one day a week at a neutral site. The youth participated voluntarily, because they wanted to work with a professional musician or choreographer, not because they wanted to mix with other races. In the process of working together on equal footing, the youth changed in small, but significant ways.

The University of California at Berkeley enjoyed a richly diverse student body in 1987. However, students tended not to mix in public places and stuck largely to their own ethnic groups. There also seemed to be few, if any, structured opportunities for students to engage in real, from-the-heart dialogue about racial and class differences. So, Stiles Hall, a 115-year-old community service agency with a historic commitment to racial justice (see index) and the Ethnic Studies Department agreed to co-sponsor an innovative, new seminar.

The original goal of the seminar, growing out of experiences with the desegregation program, was to reduce student racial isolation using an interactive three-hour semester-long seminar facilitated by an interracial team.

The focus was on genuine sharing and learning from each other's life experience in an informal, open setting—something unique to most students' experience. "Most places on campus are so competitive," one Black male wrote in his evaluation. "This is the only class I've taken that's about me, rather than what I do," wrote a White female. Indeed, many students stated that it was "the most valuable class they had taken at Cal (U.C. Berkeley)."

As part of developing a common bond, invited guest speakers, such as ex-death row inmate David McGris, Native American healer Buck Ghosthorse, Holocaust survivor Odette Meyers, and international disability rights activist Ed Roberts, captured the interest of students with their personal life stories.

Thanks to a positive reputation, students would recommend their friends for the class. It has consistently drawn one of the most diverse groups of student leaders anywhere on campus—students who are centrally involved with their representative constituencies and who often have little significant contact with those outside their group. However, even with an average forty-person waiting list for a class limited to sixteen, the project required significant outreach and recruitment each semester, in order to achieve sufficient diversity. This was particularly true with regard to privileged White male and East Asians student leaders, who have tended to be more reticent to take such a class. It was also difficult to recruit White working class students[1] and Native Americans students from the reservation, both of whom are almost non-existent at Cal and other elite Universities.

After the first three years, student feedback prompted some major changes in format. The first change entailed more time for student-to-student interaction and less time for guest speakers. In response, no outside speakers were invited and students were given structured opportunities to get to know each other more as individuals before dealing with each other as members of racial/ethnic/class groups. These opportunities included an in-depth personal introduction for each participant during the first three sessions, assigned "homework" in which pairs of students shared a favorite "hang out" and favorite piece of music with each other, and regular encouragement by the facilitators to address each other directly

---

[1]Out of the 1998 freshman class, 7 of 1127 White Freshman admitted were low-income with parents that had not attended college.

with questions. In addition, students conducted a greater percent of the course themselves. Each racial and ethnic group facilitated interactive sessions around their own experiences (i.e. Chicano/ Latinos might conduct a role play of an elementary school class entirely in Spanish—criticizing those who couldn't understand the proceedings and relating this to their own childhood experiences).

The second change was to address the underlying racial conflict earlier in the semester. Students were frustrated that genuine dialogue around racism usually occurred only in the last session or two. Consequently, instructors encouraged this, using role-plays, dyads, small groups, and discussion of readings. The instructors also alternated who was the primary person running the class, each week. This allowed the two different styles of leadership to prevail—something, which had not been as possible under the previous model of co-facilitation each week.

To help bring conflict out in the open, two "types" of student participants were helpful—students who have personally experienced the oppressive side of society and those who are clearly from a more privileged, elite background. The former type was exemplified in one class by the proud, uncompromising presence of two Native American women who grew up on reservations. Calmly, but firmly they would state, "I grew up surrounded by White people who were cruel and bigoted towards my people. I don't trust Whites and am quite suspicious of those who want to "help" us." Another example of students serving the same function were two outspoken African Americans—one of whom saw her sisters starve to death while growing up in Ghana, and the other who watched nearly all of his West Oakland peers either get killed by police, gangs, and drugs, or be jailed. They both spoke from the heart and with great humanity, while remaining uncompromising in shedding light on examples of institutional and individual racism.

The second type of student is exemplified by Ex-Governor Wilson's Northern California Youth Coordinator, who appeared on the MacNeil/Lehrer News Hour, opposing affirmative action.

He was clearly quite privileged, willing to say honestly what he thought, and open enough to others, that in the end, he admitted that he wasn't sure if he opposed affirmative action.

In sum, in order to have a genuine exchange, four key elements are necessary—elements often missing from structured "diversity experiences" on campuses.

1. Whites should be in the minority and no group should be represented by only one student. Since people in power don't "feel" their privilege, and people on the bottom don't easily share what they know when in the minority, numbers are extremely important.

2. Half the participants should be low-income or working class. Class—generally invisible in America—is the crucial missing element in most University settings.

3. Gender conflict is the most unifying and safest one to address first. Sexism must be taken seriously. Women often provide the leadership and cohesion in a group.

4. We believe that there is a hierarchy of oppression in society. Black, Chicano, and Native American working class people are at the bottom. Once racism by Whites and others against Blacks, in particular, is honestly confronted, the complexities of other intra- and inter-group prejudice can emerge.

Two key elements help structure such a diversity seminar.

1. In order to reach a truly diverse range of students—who would not normally have any real contact with each other—one must actively recruit them by establishing trust and credibility among student and staff representative of each group. They can then recommend students from that group for an interview. (We have particularly tried to recruit "leaders"—students whom their peers look up to and follow—to maximize the potential long-term impact of the seminar.)

2. Insist upon maximum participation and involvement and enforce attendance as the main course requirement. Require the students to run part of each class (with instructors' feedback, in advance) and have them assign each other "homework." Have

every student share his/her thoughts/feelings regularly in the large group, in small groups and in pairs. Throughout the semester, facilitators should find a balance between focusing on things students have in common and addressing the inevitable conflict. Generally, begin with in-depth introductions and homework assignments that allow students to get to know each other as individuals. Then look for and bring out the conflicts that evolve. Do not let your own opinions and theories dominate discussion. Share yourself, as a role model, but don't talk too much. The success of the class lies in students, themselves, taking risks with one another.

STUDENT AND FACULTY EVALUATION OF THE SEMINAR

Many of the student leaders began this seminar expressing disappointment at how racially and ethnically segregated the campus is. "Why is U.C. Berkeley a racially segregated campus despite being one of the most racially diverse in the U.S.," wrote two white females. The same feelings were echoed in a Chicano male's response. "Though I grew up in a Latino neighborhood, it's kind of sad that I have a more diverse group of friends, there, than I do at this supposedly diverse University."

Personal bonding and learning across racial and ethnic lines has been one of the most successful elements of this seminar. Many students stated in their final evaluations that this was the most valuable class they had taken at CAL. Many participants also initiated discussions and activities outside of class, affecting many more students than just those directly involved.

Another strong bond occurred between a Native American student and an African American student, who wrote, "We always joke, 'Who has it worse than we do?...Native Americans.' From this class, I see that not only do (Native Americans) still exist, but I'm committed to helping increase their numbers on this campus."

In another example, a statewide student leader and staunch opponent of affirmative action got in several heated arguments with a Black student who spoke at the Million-Man March. Later they would go out for a beer together.

Finally, a White woman, who was president of one of the most prestigious sororities at CAL, got to know the female Co-Chair of MEChA, who lived across the street at a cultural Latino house. There had been longstanding tension and a few overtly racist incidents between the mostly White upper middle class Sorority and mostly Latino working class semi-cooperative. After some heated encounters in class, the White woman volunteered, with a few other students, to serve dinner and clean up at the Latino house, as part of the Latino students' "homework assignment."

Collaborative projects across racial/ethnic lines also proved to be quite productive. One of the student leaders of the Pilipino Recruitment Project met with the student leaders of the more experienced Black Recruitment and Retention Center for advise and guidance. These and similar encounters helped create Bridges Multi-Cultural Center, now housed at Stiles Hall. The president of a prominent sorority, whose father managed a fruit packing company, accompanied the son of a farm worker for a day of work in the fields. Cal's only Latino fraternity held a joint party with the largest African American fraternity on campus, as a precursor to future joint activities.

The unique sharing across racial and ethnic lines impressed faculty who participated. Professor Ed Epstein, Chair of the Academic Senate 1988–89, remarked after sharing some of his own personal experiences with the students: "This level of open dialogue and interaction is quite rare." Professor Margaret Wilkerson, Chair of the African American Studies Department 1989–94 commented, after conducting some role-plays about interracial dating: "I wish we could clone this class across the campus." Chuck Supple, Director of the Governor's Commission on Life through Service, wrote, "These projects put Stiles Hall in the forefront of those few organizations actually addressing what may be the most crucial social issue facing campuses across the nation." David Campt, staff member of the President's Commission on Race, and former co-facilitator of the seminar, stated, "Nowhere else at the University, and perhaps in the state, have such a diversity of social, socio-economic, and political student perspectives been engaged in such a profound manner."

However, the goal of increasing students' level of commitment to institutional change does not seem to have been achieved in the short run. The personal, interactive focus of the class leaves students "unresolved about how to fight racism in the larger society," and, at least for the more privileged ones, somewhat naïve and unready to take personal responsibility for institutionalized racism. At times, we are unsure of how much interpersonal conflict to encourage and how much of a "broader context" to offer. On the one hand, people don't really change much unless issues affect them personally. On the other hand, discussions of racial and class issues in a rarified campus environment can often lose touch with broader social realities.

What we found more disturbing was the criticism that the class was structured primarily for the benefit of White students, while short-changing the learning opportunities among students of color. One African American male accused us of displaying his life in order to get guilty White students to be more sympathetic towards Black students. While these criticisms were not frequent in student evaluations, they represent important potential pitfalls.

What follows are representative narratives from students who have participated in the course over the last fifteen years. While some have clearly been quite affected by the course, others have not so obviously. The purpose of sharing their stories is both to give a three-dimensional snap-shot of the growing diversity of our society and to encourage faculty and staff from other college campuses to replicate the successful aspects of this course.

PREFACE

I grew up in a small, conservative, highly segregated Southern
California town. Mexicans lived on one side, did the dirty work,
and generally failed out of school. Whites lived on the other side
and kept the goodies for themselves. My dad, though poor growing up, made it as a corporate lawyer. My mom, though half
Jewish, hid that fact, and climbed the social ladder with my dad.
We had Black, Latino and Native American housekeepers and
babysitters. I was co-valedictorian in Junior High. With my three
blond-haired, blue-eyed brothers, we seemed like the Brady Bunch.

Then my folks divorced and things fell apart. From our
"model American family" emerged mental illness, drug addiction,
excessive debt, and gender identity issues. (However, we all also
developed into caring, decent human beings.) I escaped my family
and the town at seventeen to be an exchange student in the Neth-
erlands. My first two years at college in Santa Cruz, I fell in love
with a peer counseling program that encouraged people to cry,
and deal with race on a personal level. Later, at college in Boston,
I came out as bisexual. After obtaining a master's degree in education, I worked with a highly successful metropolitan voluntary
desegregation program for nine years. I fell in love with a feminist,
folk singer, married her and had a son, after moving back to
California. Here in Berkeley, I have worked happily for the last
fourteen years, supervising University students in mentoring and
community service, co-facilitating this seminar, and, for the last
four years, directing Stiles Hall, a non-profit community service
agency (see appendix).

Throughout my life, I have been cared for, uplifted, accepted and forgiven by people of color—especially Blacks. The women of color who helped my mom were kind to me when my stressed out, unhappy mother could not be. (I also see much of the Jewish side of my Mom—and therefore myself—in many of the Black women I have known and befriended—honest, funny, abrasive at times, and sticking up for the under-dog.) My best friend in the world grew up in Pakistan, and gave of himself in a way no White friend had ever done. My two African American bosses mentored me in a kind of fairness, even towards those you disliked, that I had never experienced among White supervisors. My closest professional colleagues are Black and Jewish. On the other hand, however, my connection to people of color is limited to work and friends. I married a middle class, White preacher's kid and live in a mostly White, urban neighborhood. I am not happy with the unearned privilege that this situation gives my family and me.

I am deeply committed to racial justice and reconciliation. I have built on a long tradition of the non-profit agency I now head, to create one of the most genuinely diverse centers on or off campus. Our 250 volunteers are a quarter Black, a quarter Latino, a quarter Asian, and a quarter White. Two-thirds of our twenty-two student employees are Black and Latino from low-income backgrounds. Our Board of Directors and staff are similarly diverse. I have organized grassroots efforts in the local school district to try to force the administration to hire more minority staff. We, the Stiles Hall Board, have also organized many Black University student, staff and faculty social and political gatherings over the years. On the other hand, I have rarely taken initiatives that might put my own personal privilege and security on the line. To be proud of myself and be able to die with dignity, I pray to have more courage to act on what I know. I share all this so that you will have a context in which to place my generalizations as to what works in setting up and carrying out a seminar dealing with race/class/gender conflict and understanding among University student leaders.

I believe that the solution to many of our most pressing social, political and environmental problems lies in a genuine human exchange on equal footing, among individuals of different racial, class and gender backgrounds. I also believe that the veil of daily, systematic discrimination experienced by women, working class people and people of color (the darker the skin, the worse the treatment), is rarely lifted and experienced by Whites, middle class adults and men. Finally, I believe that to the degree that those on both side of the veil have a genuine, equal exchange, they will become more competent, alive and human for the encounter. It is out of these beliefs and past experiences that I developed the seminar in which the students of this book participated. The course structure grew out of others' historical experiments and was continually refined and adjusted by the student participants and instructors.

Overall, we have been quite good at recruiting a diverse group of student leaders and structuring an encounter in which they could bond, engage in conflict and learn from each other. On the other hand, I feared those conflicts in the first years of the course, downplayed mixed-race and gay issues, over-categorized people, and most importantly, did not by my own example challenge students sufficiently, to confront oppression. I do believe however, that the experience has, on the whole, made a difference in the students' lives.

David Stark
Co-Instructor
General Director, Stiles Hall

It all came together that day at Il Fornaio, a trendy Italian restaurant in Burlingame. After risotto, penne, salmon, and spring salad, we settled into an engaging conversation about our childhood growing up in the southeast coastal community of St. Marys, Georgia.

We were a gathering of cousins—2 engineers, one manager, and me. Three guys and a girl, all college-educated, two of us living in the Bay Area, the other two living back in our hometown. Between ages 35 and 43, we were in the midst of our careers, three of us married and two with kids. We've traveled extensively in the Unites States and abroad. We seemed happy with our lives and talked freely about our high school, family, and friends' back home.

Because of my natural inclination to observe processes while being equally absorbed in them, it struck me that on that night we were the only black patrons in the restaurant. We were a gregarious bunch. The waiter always smiled when he came to our table and seemed to enjoy our banter as much as we did.

Then, suddenly, I got a brainstorm. If anything, this class has taught me that the only way to get to something is by going through it, that is, facing you, facing me.

"While growing up, what did we think of white people?" I asked.

"White people?"

"Where did that come from?"

"I didn't think anything about them."

"They were there."

"Yea, all over."

"Mmm, interesting question."

"In high school, we got along pretty well, it seems."

"My goodness," I said, "do we mean to say that we grew up in the 1960's and 70's in Georgia and white people were that irrelevant in our lives? How could this be?"

One of my favorite passages from Zora Neale Hurston's 1928 essay "How It Feels to Be Colored" expresses my current sentiment:

"There is no great sorrow damned up in my soul, nor lurking behind my eyes…I do not belong to the sobbing school of Negrohood who hold that nature somehow has given them a lowdown dirty deal and whose feelings are all hurt about it. Even in the helter-skelter skirmish that is my life, I have seen that the world is to the strong regardless of a little pigmentation more or less. No, I do not weep at the world—I am too busy sharpening my oyster knife."

St. Marys, Georgia, the second oldest city in the United States (it would be the oldest, but St. Augustine raced to get their charter first!), sits along the eastern seaboard, exits 1 and 2 off Interstate 95, bordering the state of Florida. I was born in Fernandina Beach, Florida about a 30-minute drive away. Boasting Jekyll, St. Simons, and Cumberland Islands (where John Kennedy and Carolyn married), the area attracts tourists year round looking for the quaint, simple life reflected in the charming, historic downtown.

The town has changed somewhat. In July 1978, President Carter installed Kings Bay Naval Submarine Support Base with the goal of supporting one squadron of Trident submarines, and about 4000 (now up to 9000) "Yankees," that is, anyone not from Georgia! This "invasion," as noted by the anti-growth sect in the community at the time, meant that our downtown family establishments—Sterling and Rowland's Grocer, Antoinette Restaurant (then the only major restaurant in town—great seafood, my first job)—would be replaced by the big multi-nationals. That is, McDonald's, Winn Dixie Grocer, and that God-awful thing that has meant the demise of high culture and class in America—the Mall!

They were right.

I came of age in a community where the teachers and principals were your parents' classmates and friends, and where the elders and the bankers were on a first-name basis. And, where on Sundays at 11, it was still the most segregated hour in America. We had no problems with that because we knew that there wasn't nothin' like black music and black preachin' and besides, there was no place else we'd rather be, except down the street to Ms. Rebecca's shop to spend our Sunday school money on candy!

St. Marys is still quite appealing despite the numerous fast food joints, Super Wal Mart, and Belk-Hudson department store. The most exclusive gated, residential golf community has black residents (my aunt among others) and counted among our more prominent citizens are black doctors, educators, and entrepreneurs.

Indeed the irony is not that racism didn't exist in my town while my cousins and I were growing up, or that a few white folks did not don white sheets every now and then. In fact, I still remember waiting in the colored section of the segregated hospital and not having access to the nicer recreation facilities in town. Rather, our parents successfully chose to keep at bay the negative impact of those very things that I have spent most of my life trying to reconcile and interpret—the intersection of race and class in America.

Up until 3rd grade, I attended an all black elementary school, Matilda Harris Elementary, named after a prominent black educator in St. Marys. Serving grades 1–7, the school was located less than one block from my home. As a first grader, I walked to school everyday with such a sense of anticipation and purpose, knowing even then that I belonged to the school and it belonged to me. My favorite memory as a second grader is when my brother's sixth grade teacher, Mrs. Baker, invited me into her class to read my brother's science book—out loud—in front of the class. It was a veil attempt to embarrass my brother for being naughty. While it may have ruined my brother's day, that incident sparked in me the notion that I was smart, and, more importantly, that I could read just as good as any sixth grade boy!

Sadly, all that would soon change.

Because of the closure of Matilda Harris Elementary in 1971 (the 1954 Brown v. Board of Education decision finally caught up with our town), I began fourth grade at the local St. Marys Elementary—the heretofore all white school. Some of the teachers at Matilda were relocated to St. Marys Elementary. Thank goodness. To this day, I am grateful for the stern disposition of Ms. Mary Jane Stevens—a look or simple glance was all that was needed to let us know that she meant business. Black kids and white kids—we knew that when we entered her space, learning was about to take place.

But to no surprise, it was just not the same. With *some* white teachers, I was often overlooked when I raised my hand, was told on many occasions that I talked too much, that I should stick to spelling because I was not good in math. I learned more about what I was not good at, than learning more about my natural talents. I became bitter and disillusioned. Interestingly, it is only upon current reflection that I'm able to make the connection between my move to a lesser accommodating school and my subsequent disinterest in the learning process which, incidentally, I've successfully turned around as indicated by my chosen profession in higher education.

I started high school in 1975. Camden County High had also been integrated four years earlier, and by the time I arrived, the black principal from the all black high school in the county had become the principal. That, I believe, made all the difference in the world.

Peter J. Baker was from the Benjamin Mays tradition. A black man on a mission, he was the symbol of excellence and achievement for many of the black kids in the county. He personified perfection and did not expect anything less from his students. One can call it fear, but we were highly motivated to come to school, be in class by the ringing of the bell, go to class, stay in class, and carry our hall pass. There was nothing more frightening than being caught in the hallway without a pass. Mr. Baker would stand at a very strategic intersection in the hall where he could see north, south, east, west, around corners, in nooks and crannies—he was everywhere and saw everything. And don't think that just because he was having a conversation with someone while standing there that he wouldn't see you. Big mistake.

I clearly remember the time I had to pass him in the hallway to get to my class. About half way there, the bell rang. I naively assumed that because Mr. Baker would see me hustling that I'd be left alone. Not only did he stop to reprimand me, he went on about how he graduated from high school with my mom, that she, my dad, nor my aunts and uncles would approve of my tardiness, that being late is disrespectful to the people waiting, that it would instill bad character, and so on.

His words still ring in my ear as I hustle from one campus meeting to another.

My high school experience was the healing I needed after the psychological bruising in the elementary school. I developed into a confident and ambitious young woman. I graduated with honors and went on to attend a prestigious, church-affiliated, private school in middle Georgia—the first black student from my county to attend Mercer University. And yes, it was a black school counselor—Mr. Rhodes—who encouraged me to apply. Ironically, the principal of my white elementary school was a graduate of Mercer. I feel like I should say something about poetic justice, but I'm not one to gloat.

It was through time spent in southern Africa and the Caribbean that I began to see myself as part of the dynamic Diaspora of black people in the world. Upon graduation from Mercer and with the financial assistance of the University and the black Masonic Lodge in St. Marys, I spent the summer of 1983 in Lesotha, southern Africa, a tiny country completely surrounded by the then apartheid Republic of South Africa. It served as a hide-a-way for the then outlawed African National Congress and had been bombed by the Republic just days before I arrived. In fact, while having lunch in downtown Maseru, a car bomb exploded less than a block away and shattered the restaurant window.

Young and optimistically naive, I remained in the country to complete the building of the elementary school in northern Lesotha, Kolo Ha Ntsie. Later, I coordinated similar work projects in the eastern Caribbean, working with a multicultural mix of high school students from across America and their counterparts on the islands of Barbados, St. Vincent, Antigua, Montserrat, Grenada, and the Cariacou Islands. Here was an early introduction of ethnic and gender exploration through meaningful engagement with one another, while also doing work that benefited the local communities.

I was interested in exploring black identity within the context of other third world peoples rather than within the existing paradigm of white domination.

No doubt that my experiences in these predominately black countries helped to shape my decision to live in a place where I would see, with regularity, the plethora of cultures, religions, and lifestyles that I had come to value throughout my travels. What better place than in California? What better city than Berkeley? And what better institution but the University of California, Berkeley?

This seminar—Ethnic Studies 198—has allowed for arguably one of the most exhaustive and complex explorations of the practical engagement of diversity on any college campus. I am able to observe sixteen pre-selected inquiring and unyielding student leaders struggle with what it means—not to mention what it would take—to live in a truly pluralistic society. I am struck by how easy I considered "taking up arms" after listening to powerful and persuasive oratory by a black man who believes that a class war is inevitable. Or how quick I was to anger upon hearing from a student, with such conviction, that he had no use for his parent's native language. The views and the subsequent passion run the gamut. They speak with the privilege of a ruling elite class and with the suffocating struggles of a newly arrived immigrant. The students are indeed brilliant, morose, acrimonious, sanguine, and triumphant—without contradiction or apology.

And yes, the world also belongs to these strong-minded students as they sharpen their own oyster knives in preparation for their life's work toward social justice and social change. And it also belonged to my family in southeast Georgia as they chose to instill in us cousins the value of black self-reliance, regardless of anyone else's agenda to the contrary.

Jerlena D. Griffin
Co-Instructor
Director, Residential Living
and New Student Services

INTRODUCTION

In some important ways, the Stiles Hall experiment could be legitimately called *The Diversity Project, Phase Two.*

In 1991, a team of researchers from the Institute for the Study of Social Change issued a report on the ways in which undergraduate students at the Berkeley campus of the University of California were adjusting to enrollments that made for sharply increasing ethnic, racial, and cultural diversity. The report of their experiences was entitled *The Diversity Project.* It was widely distributed locally on the campus and to California institutions, but it also went out, upon request, to more than eighty colleges and universities around the country (and several abroad). Indeed, the fact that the study's results were reported on the front pages of the *New York Times,* and highlighted by the BBC, CNN, Australian, French, Greek and Canadian television helps explain why *The Diversity Project* went through two printings of 5,000 copies.

What was the appeal? While there is no quick and simple answer, I do believe that the most important explanation is directly related to why the material in this book will also have a strong appeal. The early report did two things. First, it provided a substantial megaphone for the voices of hundreds of students in the experience of the day-to-day "dealing with" campus ethnic, racial and cultural diversity. Some of the results were counter intuitive and a challenge to the conventional wisdom. Because of patterns of residential segregation in the United States, elementary and high schools are predominantly racially segregated. Freshman arriving in the late 1980s and early 1990s came to the campus expressing high hopes about the advantages and attraction of coming to "such a diverse" campus. As noted in the *Diversity Project's* opening pages, at least 75 per cent of students from all backgrounds answered a freshman survey by saying that "they came to Berkeley because they so strongly favored the diversity" of the campus. Then after four or five years on campus, one could routinely find seniors who were frustrated about what they perceived to the "self-segregation" of the various groups and who lamented what they saw as a missed opportunity.

The counter-intuitive finding was the second accomplishment. That is, the report attempted to explain some of the social forces behind this perception of "self segregation." It did this in large part by reporting on how the early encounters in their transition from high school to college shaped their experiences, and in part by providing a relatively focused social science lens on patterns of affiliation.

As principal investigator, I was frequently invited to speak about the project in many different venues across the country, and I was always struck by how common were the themes that students addressed at Berkeley, whether at small liberal arts colleges or at large urban universities; whether at Hunter College in New York or Hastings College in Hastings, Nebraska. Berkeley may have been one of the first major campuses to go through the substantial reshaping of the ethnic and racial composition of its student body, but the issues raised were echoed on campuses that were nowhere nearly as diverse. A few years ago, Beverly Tatum even published a book on one aspect of this phenomenon, *Why Are All the Black Kids Sitting Together in the Cafeteria: And Other Conversations About Race.*

It is in this context that we come to Stiles Hall, and why the program there is some version of Diversity Project II. One of the recommendations was that students should be assigned joint projects related to curricular issues. Since the curriculum was the core enterprise of academic life, it was here that the university could play a more significant role in helping students achieve their own stated goals of "engaging" their diversity. What Native American and

African American students were most likely to mean by "engaging diversity," however, involved some sharp changes in organizational and institutional practices. White students, on the other hand, were more likely to mean by "engaging diversity" that there be more personal interactions and possible friendships. The gap was substantial, and a substantial part of the explanation for the surface appearance of self-segregation. The recommendation to engage students in collective activities was designed to help bridge that gap.

Institutions and organizations are very slow to change their practices, and colleges and universities are no exception. The Berkeley campus did introduce a curricular innovation called the American Cultures Requirement, and over the last decade more than 400 courses have been transformed to have more comparative features. Many of these courses have done a better job than other academic courses of helping students to "engage" issues of diversity. It is Stiles Hall, however, where one can see the effect of a more systematic approach.

The appeal of this book will come from its heavy and appropriate reliance upon the rich texture of very divergent student positions—provided in *the voices of those students in the experience*. Typical classrooms are lacking in substantial exchange or encounters among and between students. Indeed, as Paolo Friere described, one-way communication evolves out of a model where the instructor sees his or her primary role as pouring information into "empty vessels" (students).   There is not much time for, and often less patience for, and interactionist model of learning. In contrast, Stiles Hall, just at the edge of the Berkeley campus, is the dramatic exception. Here, students both meet and interact through joint projects in behalf of social justice, or through more modest interventions (e.g., tutoring students in a very different part of town). Such collective enterprises are unique. There was no mere encounter for encounter's sake, no "student version" of *The Color of Fear* (a movie where a group of men confront each other about their personal concerns about racial relations—but have no other engagement with each other outside the borders of that room). Rather, the students at Stiles have a genuine engagement with both the world, and with each other, and the leadership of the program has made certain that they have the structured framework in which to reflect upon the inter-connection between the parts.

In that sense, the Stiles Hall experiment goes one step beyond *Skin Deep*, a film which is one of the richest portraitures of inter-personal engagement among college students, but which had the limitation of students only being together for a brief few days. In contrast, the Stiles Hall situation permits a kind of ongoing probing and reflection that is the fertile grounds for generating a genuine shift in understanding and perception. This comes through in many of the self-reported stories of what these young adults were "going through." What the reader will get from these accounts is a textured account of the triumphs and the failures of engaging people across large chasms. Social change is often a slow and painful process, especially when disrupting deep and unexamined assumptions and routine practices. But rather than taking my word for it, the reader is much further advanced by hearing directly from those in the process.

Troy Duster
Director, Center for the Teaching
and Study of American Cultures
Professor Emeritus of Sociology

Chicano/Latino

"I was the first in my extended family to go to college. To go back home was to sink, and I was not going to let that happen. I had to pave the college path for my younger siblings."

—Hector, Fall 1997

Hector

I grew up in a poor neighborhood in Los Angeles composed mainly of Mexican and Chinese immigrant families. My parents had settled there during the early 70's when they illegally migrated across the border to the U.S. from their poverty-stricken towns in Mexico in search of "dolares." They had met in the workplace where they assembled handbags for a small business in the downtown area. I was the product of an unsettling desire for personal gratification, an accident as they call me.

Life in Lincoln Heights was fun for a kid. Everyday I played with my school friends who lived in the same block or down the street. Games of tackle football in the middle of the street, and freeze tag fill my memory of my own personal wonder years. But life for my parents was difficult. The job at the factory in downtown did not amount to much, so my father started a business as a carpenter in the hopes of making more money. The business lasted only a few years; however, it was long enough for my father to save money and fulfill his and my mother's long lost dream: The dream of returning to the homeland.

We moved to Mexico when I was eleven, and settled in a very small town in the state of Zacatecas. Our lives had completely changed over night. In Los Angeles we were lower class, barely made the equivalent to minimum wage for a family of five. But in Mexico the savings tripled due to the currency exchange. We were actually a part of the middle class in that town. My mother did not have to work any more because my father had started the same business in Mexico, and had tremendous success. Life had taken a turn, and my parents had never been happier.

I, on the other hand, was confused. I had never felt such a feeling of disorientation. I became aware that I was not the same as my fellow classmates because I was raised in the United States, because I thought and acted like a gringo; the bottom line was that I was not considered Mexican. I understood that I could not adopt the Mexican identity, because of my upbringing. I was a pocho, a Chicano, a gringo, and a guero, but not a Mexican. I came to the realization that having Mexican parents, and command of the Spanish language, was not enough to consider myself as a Mexicano. I had been exposed to a different world, a world that only the privileged wealthy families in the town were able to afford. Nonetheless, I enjoyed a privileged lifestyle due to the blessing that my family was well off. I had no worries, and I was very glad that I did not have to hold a job during my middle school years as so many of my friends did. They paved the streets, plowed their farms, picked tunas (cactus fruit), or worked with the meat vendors in the market place for a living. I was fortunate I could go home and study. Of course I took my privilege for granted; I never had to question it because that's just the way things were. I was never even aware of it; it was a state of uninterrupted bliss.

We moved back to the U.S. and relocated in Moreno Valley, a suburb of Riverside California so that I can finish my high school education. An aunt welcomed us to live in her garage as we rebuilt our lives in the U.S., and my parents looked for a job. My experience that first year back in the United States was disturbing, I was called a wetback by White and Black students on campus and was spat at on my way home from school by a car full of White guys. Both groups would also constantly harass me. I did not know what to make of my situation, how to act, or what crowd I was welcomed in. The Black and White students did not make me feel comfortable because I generalized the actions of a few and made assumptions of the rest. My only way out was to hang out with the Chicanos on campus. They were my safety net because we looked alike and shared the same cultural experiences. They made me feel secure, and accepted me for who I was. I was not a wetback with them, and I felt a common bond of protecting each other from the White and Black students.

My disillusionment with those who I shared camaraderie came when the racists remarks were made by my friends to Black, White, Asian, and everyone else who was not of Mexican descent. I found it very confusing to see my safety net fall from under me, and found it disheartening that I could not make any other friends for fear of being shoved aside because of what the color of my skin, my broken English, and my high cheek bones represented. What is a small town boy who recently came from Mexico to know of the racial intolerance in this country? I knew I was not Mexican because that was made clear to me in Mexico, and I knew I was not American because those who denied my phenotypic characteristics to be associated with that identity spit on me. In short, I felt a deep resentment for both cultures. I felt anger towards the Mexico who I felt was supposed to embrace me, and I felt betrayed by the American Dream, that dream which was drilled into us in grammar school as we recited daily the pledge of allegiance.

I realized that the dream would be limited to me because there are those who guard it against foreigners. I knew that whatever I identified myself with I would always be in between two very distinct worlds. Aside from keeping a close-knit friendship with the Chicano crowd I was very fortunate to acquire many friendships with Blacks and White students from my classes. But I am guilty of a fault. I grew up thinking of Black culture as very different from mainstream American culture. Perhaps my judgement was obscured by what I saw on television, and in the movies. I never knew how American my Black friends were. By American I refer to the cultural knowledge, the loyalty to the corporate American ideal, and the prejudices, against foreigners, akin to those many whites hold. For example, having a wave of Mexican immigrant families into Moreno Valley was not as welcomed by the White or Black families that were already established in that city. Some of that intolerance was manifested in the race riots on campus, or the racial insults from White and Black elders towards my parents in the supermarket.

Culturally speaking, I was surprised to experience that many of my Black friends were so American. In the Mexican culture, the family structure is very communal, hence the reason we were living in a garage until we were financially stable. I experienced that many of my Black friends only looked out for themselves in class and while playing sports. How selfish, I used to think. If in a situation where I felt another student needed help either in class or out on the football field, I would go out of my way to lend a hand. I did not understand why Americans in general (Whites and Blacks) could be so egotistic, and I translated that cultural attribute as rude and inconsiderate. I must admit that I was more disappointed with my first experience with Blacks because I expected that as non-white Americans, they would understand the hardships of other non-white Americans such as myself. Why can't I speak Spanish in the hallways without being criticized by non-Spanish speaking students (Blacks and Whites)? As far as my experience with White students, I expected such an experience. It did not surprise me that I felt so disconnected to their lifestyle. As a kid I had convinced myself that the White American culture was a completely different world from mine, and I did not care to understand it because it was never pertinent to my survival. I never cared about Marcia and Greg's problems on the Brady Bunch, or why Roscoe and Boss Hog felt it was necessary to pursue the Dukes. That was not important in my life, and what I cared about was never even on English-speaking network television. I only spent one year in that high school, and actually ended up graduating from a predominantly Latino populated high school in Los Angeles.

When I was accepted into U.C. Berkeley, I imagined that my educational experience would be incomparable to the misguided and mediocre education that I received from the public school system in Los Angeles. No doubt, the academic experience was more than I expected from another public school system. I was exposed to the best professors, cutting edge research, and countless intellectually stimulating opportunities. But the student life at Cal was worse than I had ever experienced. Blunt comments such as "there goes an affirmative action student" by White students were very frequent and other remarks from Whites and Asians such as "immigrants are taking resources away from American citizens" filled me with both anger and resentment towards those intolerant groups of students. In my experience, these comments were only directed at the Chicano/Latino and Black students on campus, and were directed by White and Asians.

I was hesitant to disclose information about my high school GPA and SAT for fear of confirming that I was an affirmative action student. Being Chicano was bad enough, and if I did not have perfect SAT scores and GPA, I must be unqualified. I believed that it was only the freshman class that was this ignorant; I believed that upperclassmen were different, more mature. However, that was not the case either. Stories of beatings on Black students by White mobs at night filled me with terror as I walked to the dorms alone at night. Although I am not Black, as a Chicano, I became aware that the Black and Latino experiences in Berkeley were similar. The negative stigma of affirmative action seemed to affect every ethnic group on campus with the exception of some Asian students. We became the people of color on campus, and were drawn to each other by the common experience of fighting the unjust stereotype that was directed towards us. This experience as a person of color was what made me fear walking alone at night. If a Black was targeted, it was only a matter of time before the Chicano/Latino, and other ethnic communities fell victim to the same threats. To say I was disillusioned with my Berkeley experience is to put it lightly. I was disgusted. I did not understand how the most highly educated students in the nation could be so ignorant and foolish.

I was so unhappy with my life at Berkeley that I began to doubt my very potential to succeed academically. Maybe I was not smart enough or maybe the admissions office made a mistake in accepting me. How could I be here if I never even considered going to college when considering my future in high school? I was lucky when a high school counselor pulled me aside my junior year and rearranged my whole schedule of classes with the purpose of making me UC eligible. Even when it came time to applying in my senior year, the only reason I completed the application was because it was a mandatory assignment for my AP English class. It was just an accident; I thought I got into Berkeley on sheer luck.

I had let the situation get the best of me. I even considered transferring to UCLA my second year to be closer to my family and away from all this animosity. But I was faced with two realities that year. In Lincoln High School, I had been unexposed to any sort of racial and cultural intolerance. The school was mainly composed of first generation Chinese and Mexicans, and both groups lived in relative harmony. Either group against the other made no serious threats. I had deliberately blocked from my mind the hostile racial environment I had experienced before. People's prejudices were not going to change no matter where I went, and just because UCLA was in Los Angeles there is a big difference between Lincoln Heights and West LA. My own family were themselves racist, I remembered. When my grandmother along with all my father's sisters first laid eyes on my mother, they resented her because of her dark skin. I was given special treatment from my

Grandmother and aunts because I was lighter than my brother and sister, and this came without an assumption. The other reality was that I was the first in my extended and immediate family to go to college, and that all eyes were on me to either sink or swim. To go back home was to sink, and I was not going to let that happen. I had to pave the college path for my younger siblings.

Looking back, I regret letting those negative experiences affect my judgement. The only way I was able to overcome the hostility was by taking a proactive approach towards cultural and racial harmony on campus. I did not want to react anymore. I wanted some answers. In my search for justice I found Stiles Hall and the Ethnic Studies course which would eventually quell my anger and frustration. I also became involved in student government by holding a Senate seat, and getting involved with the Cal-SERVE political party whose mission is to represent the underrepresented on campus.

The course was one of the best I ever took at Cal. To have students from all walks of life in the same room was progress in a campus that self segregates itself into racial and cultural cliques. The key ingredient in my positive experience with the course was the structure of the curriculum. We learned from each other's life experiences, and our homework involved personal social activities with others from different cultural groups in class. This was positive because we were given full reign of what we could share and learn. What was difficult about this structure was that the constant fear of coming off as a racist or a culturally insensitive bigot did not allow us to share honest opinions in the beginning. The group was very careful in choosing what to say for fear of offending anybody. This environment made it very difficult to encourage an open debate on issues surrounding race.

Our conversations were very superficial in the beginning of the semester, but got exciting as our reaction to one another's comments touched on very sensitive nerves. To feel attacked when others would touch on sensitive issues was a very natural reaction, because we all began to question each other's lifestyle, and to question each other's lifestyle is to make a slight judgement on our upbringing. Something that was very hard for some people to handle, considering many of us felt we had great values and beliefs that we were not willing to change. One experience that haunts me involved one White student being related to a Nazi German official who served during Hitler's reign. This student never had a clue about her relation to such a relative until she confronted her mother as a teenager when she heard rumors of the relationship. Apparently her grandfather had been a member of the Nazi party and held a rank in the military. She questioned why it was a secret in the family, and was given the reason—shame. What was interesting was that she understood why it was important to conceal such information from younger siblings. When I asked whether she would continue this practice, to my surprise she responded, yes. She would hide this fact from her future children because it was unnecessary information, she explained. As expected we questioned her line of reasoning and shared our concerns about how important it was to be honest about her ancestry. There is no doubt our questions made her feel tremendously uncomfortable, because as far as she was concerned, her belief system was valid, and what was important was that her mother supported and practiced such a belief system.

This was the most challenging hurdle that I am fortunate to have experienced. Nobody wants to be told that the way they were brought up and the values ingrained in their subconscious are wrong. Those values and beliefs shape our character and outlook on life. To have anybody challenge those beliefs on the grounds that they are racist or culturally biased leads to a practice in self-denial. Nobody wants to admit that his or her belief system is inherently wrong. Herein lies the foolishness of the typical White Cal student I encountered.

What is wrong with an intellectual conversation that challenges our belief system? Is not this why we are pursuing a college education? If I mention that your cultural values infringe on my personal life experience as a person of color, is it to attack your belief system? I simply want to open your mind to the reality of White privilege in America. I feel screwed, and historically you have been doing the screwing. So forgive me if I want your family to feel shame over the racist and cruel practices your grandfather exposed himself to. So suck it up, and learn from it because I am not going to have my children spit on by your sons or daughters who unknowing to them have the racist hatred ingrained in their subconscious simply because you would not address it with them for fear of feeling shame. Your silence is part of the problem, because until you share your prejudices we will not begin to understand whether your beliefs are based on stereotypes or on realities. Of course these are unspoken comments I was unable to communicate due to anger and frustration. I regret not being able to explain how the silence expressed by the student with the Nazi ancestor filled me with a sense of rage.

Frankly, it took time before I realized that my opinions are as valid as her sensitivity regarding her belief system. I actually felt bad for her when our line of questioning ensued, but with time I have learned that my experience as a person of color cannot be silenced in order to make someone else feel uncomfortable. The experiences in the class shocked me sometimes. We explored provocative topics like the issues surrounding Affirmative Action and Proposition 209, Immigrant Rights, and Proposition 187, the reason why minority groups protest so much on campus, and our own personal life stories surrounding our prejudices, to name a few. But the topics always revolved around questions we (the Chicano, Black, and Native American students) had of the White and Asian students. We wanted to know how they perceived our protests and our lifestyle, but I felt their answers were limited and well thought out. I did not want them to think; I just wanted them to answer with their gut instinct and anger about what they believed in. There was no way we were going to be able to face our differences unless we were completely honest with each other. But throughout the semester we continued the process of trying to break down the barrier of fear that I felt the White and Asian students had—fear of sounding racist maybe, or fear of not being able to express their true feeling without offending anybody in the room. But that was exactly the opposite of why I was there. I wanted all of us to face that fear so that we could begin to explore its origin and discuss what we could do about it so that we can all begin to coexist in harmony.

When a few would finally reach that point of brutal honesty the conversation usually ended in tears. Something I was guilty myself, and tried to avoid such conversations. Brutal honest comments like, "why don't you shut up, work hard, and stab whitey in the back once you're in a position of power," as shared by an Asian male drove me to anger and tears. I wanted to slap him around the room so that I can knock some sense into him about the realities that people of color experience in life and in Berkeley in particular. I wanted to make him understand that as an Asian male, he himself was a target of white privilege, because immigrants come in all shapes and sizes, and American society makes it clear that whoever immigrants are, they are not White. His ignorance on this issue came from his experience as a third generation Asian, I thought to myself. He will continue to be blind to the realities as long as he is at Berkeley enjoying the beneficial stereotype of being a smart Asian. However, if he was somewhere in Riverside, his ass would be running away from the hatred others would gladly bestow upon him, because at first sight, most see an Asian as not an American. This was another topic we were unable to explore in depth, but that I really wanted to pursue.

Furthermore, I was concerned with the distinction among Asians. In my experiences in Senate and with Recruitment and Retention Centers on campus, Southeast Asians and Asian Pacific Islanders also felt as people of color on campus. This experience as an involved student on campus frustrated the hell out of me when policies such as the minority scholarship we established was attacked on grounds that it included Asians as minorities on campus. A Daily Cal article states, "Asians are the single largest group on campus, Clearly this scholarship discriminates only against Whites." How ignorant is that! The Asian population on campus is composed of a diverse population of individuals, many of who have roots in the countries of the Asian continent. To include southeast Asians and Asian Pacific Islanders in the scholarship was to acknowledge that their representation in the student population was dismal, not to discriminate against Whites.

These are concerns I wanted to understand, and an area I wanted to explore with everyone in the class. That did not happen. The class seemed to drag at times, and seemed to get nowhere. The anger in everyone's eyes filled the room with a thick tension guarded by a wall of silence. There were comments at times that would make me think that it was hopeless to ever understand each other's differences or even begin to want to understand. Comments like, "we don't have to support those who come as immigrants," as uttered by a White female regarding Proposition 187, were not taken lightly. Many lashed out in anger while others were mute with rage. But by the end of the day we were exhausted and lacked answers about how to address our differences without screaming or crying. I always remember questioning what I was learning in the class, and could not put my finger on it. After all, the Chicanos, Blacks, and Native Americans were always communicating with the Whites and Asians about how we lived our lives and why we did the things that we did. I never seemed to understand their perspective, because it always seemed guarded.

I realized what my purpose in the class was when the Chicano students did an exercise that involved personal references that we wanted to share with the class. Each sentence started with "I want you to know…" and followed with a personal comment on anything we wished to share. I wanted them to know that as a kid I was confused when I thought I was White and my mother Black as I observed that my skin tone was lighter than my mother's. I wanted them to know that growing up with light skin among Chicanos was full of privilege. Family members and strangers constantly called me guero (white boy), followed by "he has such fair skin, he must be adopted." I felt anger when my brother and sister were treated differently by my family members and friends because of their darker skin, as many claimed I could not be related to them. I wanted them to know that I felt resentment towards the cultural intolerance of being a recent immigrant from Mexico, and that I was not a wetback. I wanted them to know that the American dream was a nightmare for people of color, because of the cultural values on which it is based. I was not going to stop lending a hand only to advance my personal career.

Most importantly, I wanted the White students to fucking listen. I wanted them to listen to our gripes and criticisms, and I wanted them to open up to criticism and not blind themselves with denial. Many of their parents were irresponsible in planting the seed of racial/cultural intolerance by not addressing with them the differences among Americans. As we shared our most intimate issues with this diverse group of students, I realized that what we were trying to get across was more than our beliefs and experiences. We were trying to interrupt that uninterrupted state of bliss that the White students were not even aware they possessed. We were trying to make them think of the privilege that came with being White and affluent. The privilege we knew we did not possess but fought to gain as we marched on in countless protests against referendums like Proposition 187 and 209.

They blindly ignored their privilege because it has always been with them since birth, and has never been challenged or uninterrupted until now. All I wanted was for them to acknowledge that they were privileged, and to understand that we cannot ignore our racial/cultural differences. Our differences are what make this country strong, and promising. To ignore those differences is a practice in social irresponsibility. Our efforts were not as influential as we would hope because interrupting their state of bliss challenged their values and belief system. So they retreated behind a wall of silence as we screamed and cried about the simple realization we wanted them to make.

I learned that I could not shake their belief system. I learned that they would guard it against all odds when challenged. I can no longer ignore the White American cultural ideals that I once believed were not pertinent to my survival. As an educated person of color living in the United States at the turn of the 21st Century, I am as responsible to shake off the state of uninterrupted bliss that blinds many from the reality that people of color experience daily. This state of mind has for too long ignored our people's cry for social justice and equality. Furthermore, the cultural intolerance among people of color is another obstacle that we must overcome if we are to unite in the struggle towards an equal society. Blacks, Chicanos, Mexicanos, Latinos, Native Americans, and Asians of all nationalities must become aware that our welfare is in jeopardy in this divisive country. As people of color we must strive to elevate our communities towards educational, political and economic empowerment so that our collective voice can interrupt that state of privilege many have enjoyed at our expense.

For new students, you are about to embark on a journey that will challenge the belief system that makes you an individual. You will be challenged mentally, physically, and spiritually, but beware. The wealth of knowledge found in the textbooks will only cause a dent in your vessel of knowledge. The life experiences of those around you will rock and pitch your insignificant ship, and ultimately destroy it if you are willing to listen and open yourself up to criticism. My recommendation: listen, let go of that raft you believe is your salvation. Let it be destroyed because it is not strong enough to handle the currents of truth and wisdom. Only hold on to the pieces that remind you of why you began the journey in the first place. Don't be foolish and ignore the truth others have to offer for fear of leaving that comfort zone. If you find that Berkeley is a great academic institution and that you have never been happier, then you are either the eternal embodiment of truth or you are a simple-minded fool. For those of you who associate yourselves as White Americans, let me be the first to let you know that you hold a position of privilege in this society just because you are White. First, I want you to accept this, and second I want you to recognize that you do not deserve this. You must also be tolerant of other ethnic groups on campus; they are key to your educational experience at Cal. For the student of Asian descent, you must do your ethnic group a favor and clarify your nationality or cultural identity. This country is obsessed with classifying anybody with slanted eyes as Asian. Carve your identity and demand that you are identified with your rightful group, and if you are unwilling to pursue this practice then demand they call you American. For the people of color, the Chicanos, Blacks, Native Americans, etc. be prepared to fight, fight, fight. Assume nobody is willing to support you and strengthen your cause in numbers. Support each other in every march, protest or sit-in. Let me let you in on a little secret: you are no longer an individual, but part of a group. To everyone, everybody on this campus is as or more qualified and intelligent than you, so do not look like an idiot by showing off your high school grades and SAT scores. That information is now irrelevant. One more thing, you should all take at least one Ethnic Studies class so that you can learn the real history of this nation.

Frances

Spring 1997

All four of my grandparents were born and raised in Puerto Rico. As far as they know, their parents and grandparents were also born and raised on the island. My paternal grandfather, Papa Chin, says his father's mother came to Puerto Rico from Spain. She's the only ancestor that I can trace back to the "Old World." But just by looking at my grandparents you can tell that they all have mixes of African, European, and Native blood that make up the Puerto Rican nation.

My mother was also born and raised on the island, in a beautiful mountainous town called San Sebastian. She was one of seven children, and her parents were very poor farmers. She has the great stories of walking barefoot for miles, over creeks and through farms to get to school. She says all her brothers and sisters had two pairs of shoes, one for school (which they only put on when they got to school), and one for church. They were so poor, that they never took pictures. The earliest picture I have ever seen of mami is at age fifteen.

My father's story is very different. Papa Chin joined the military during WWII and then moved to New York after the war. As most Puerto Ricans who leave our enchanted yet impoverished island, he was an economic refugee. He was forced to leave Puerto Rico to survive. So my father and his siblings were born in Queens, New York. My grandfather worked long hours and any overtime possible to provide a good living for his family. My grandmother, Mama Luz, also worked. They saved enough money to buy a house in Long Island, a suburb of New York. So papi grew up in a working class family, with many more opportunities than mami. There are a lot of pictures of papi growing up. I've even seen pictures of him when he was just a baby.

The first time I can remember feeling different because I am Puerto Rican was in third grade. I had just moved to San Diego from the island, and I did not know English very well. I was in a regular third grade class, but I was pulled out a few hours everyday to work with an ESL teacher. But at that time, it was just the language thing that made me feel different. I didn't think much about the fact that my culture was also very different. I was always proud of my culture. The first time I remember feeling different because of my culture was back in Puerto Rico, when kids called me "gringa" because I spoke English and had lived in the states. That really hurt, because I didn't feel different from them; I always felt 100% Boricua.

Class was the thing I noticed first. During my second grade year I was living with Mama Luz and Papa Chin in my hometown, Yauco, Puerto Rico. That year we moved from our house in the country, to a house in Colinas, an urbanized area in town. In the country, we were well off compared to our neighbors. We had a cement house with a bathroom inside the house and we even had a car. But in Colinas, we were poorer than our neighbors were, most of whom were doctors, teachers, and other professionals. I remember feeling different when I couldn't go with my friends to see Menudo in concert because the tickets cost too much. Instead, Papa Chin would walk me to the coliseum when the concert had already begun, and we would hear the shows from outside. Sometimes he would convince someone at the door to let us step inside, so we could actually see some of the show.

I was fortunate to grow up both in Yauco and in San Diego, California. I also lived for a short time in Atlanta, Georgia and in Long Island, New York. Growing up, I resented moving around so much. I moved back and forth between Yauco and San Diego a lot. I usually only stayed in one place for two years at a time. But when I got to college, I finally realized that I was lucky to have moved so much. Unlike most Puerto Ricans raised in California, I identified strongly with Puerto Rico, our people, and our culture. I understand the reality of Puerto Rican life because I have lived and studied on the island. I always knew what it meant to be Boricua, and I was always very proud of my heritage. Although I lived in places where there were few Boricuas and almost no knowledge of Puerto Rico and its people, I never suffered a cultural identity crisis. In San Diego everyone thought I was Mexican, and in Georgia people thought I was Black and White. Whenever someone questioned my heritage, I was happy to tell anyone about my island and my culture. I never get tired of explaining my Boricua heritage. I actually enjoy it!

I always knew I wanted to go to college. By the time I was in eighth grade, I couldn't wait to get to college. In eleventh grade,

I finally went on a school college trip. We took a bus all the way to Berkeley, stopping at various college campuses along the way. It was the first time I saw other universities besides UCSD and SDSU. The first time I saw Berkeley, I hated it. I thought it was ugly and dirty, and the bay area weather sucked. I had my heart set on UCLA, but for no reason at all. Luckily, the adults that I worked with at San Diego Youth and Community Services encouraged me to seriously consider Berkeley. One of my favorite teachers, a Cal alum, also encouraged me to go to Berkeley. My mom didn't know the difference between Cal and San Diego State, so she couldn't give me much advice. Finally, on the weekend before I had to make my final decision, a friend and mentor flew me up to the Bay Area, rented us a car, and showed me around. She wanted to show me that the Bay Area had many different sides; it wasn't all like Telegraph Avenue. I also got to stay with a friend of ours who was then a freshman at Cal. I got to see first hand what living in Berkeley was like, and that's what finally won me over!

The five years I spent at Cal were some of best years of my life. I had such a great time. I can't believe how much I grew. I learned so much, not only in my classes (I actually learned little there!) but also from my environment, my peers, and the movements that were going on during those years (the battle to save affirmative action, Propositions 209,187, 227, etc.). I also met a group of Puerto Rican students that became my closest friends. Together we formed a Puerto Rican student group called Acción Boricua y Caribeña (Puerto Rican and Caribbean Students in Action), a.k.a. ABC. We were from all over the diaspora, some of us were 100% Boricua; some of us were mixed. But it was an amazing thing, because we were mostly at the same level of political consciousness. The one thing most of us had in common was that we had little knowledge about Puerto Rican history, and even less about Puerto Rican politics and current issues. But we all had a common desire to learn more. We organized a De-Cal class to learn more about these issues. With guidance from graduate students and professors from all over the country and from the island, we created a syllabus for the class. We began by studying the native peoples of the island, the Tainos, and went all the way up to present day issues and struggles. After the De-Cal class we organized trips to the East Coast and to Southern California, and we held many educational forums and protests at Cal. I had the best times with the folks from ABC, and they are now part of my family.

During my fourth year at Cal, I took the race relations class through Stiles Hall. A lot of my friends had taken the class and said it was a really amazing experience. Since I was a Political Science and Rhetoric major, I rarely had the opportunity to discuss issues of race and alliance building in any of my courses. Even worse, there was no space to openly discuss my views on political issues. Both departments are pretty conservative, and I often got ridiculed for speaking up in class. I looked forward to taking the class at Stiles where open and honest discussion about difficult, but important, issues was not only welcomed, but also encouraged. As a matter of fact, openness and honesty were the foundations of the class. We all wanted to reach some kind of understanding, to find a common ground. We knew that we could not move forward unless we were absolutely open and honest about our beliefs, feelings, and misconceptions around issues of class and race. We also knew that the process required each of us to tell our own stories in our voices. What I value most about this class is the rare opportunity to share my story and to hear others' stories, to discuss honestly and openly our ideas about race and class, and to attempt to build alliances across cultural differences.

My most memorable experience in the class was also my most painful. I remember when the Chicano and Latino students in class gave an assignment to the White students. Their task was to go to the Chicano Latino theme house, Casa Juaquin Murieta, and work for an evening as "the help." They had to serve the Latino residents of the house and then clean up after them. In the next class the White students reported about their experience. A few things really stood out for me about that exercise. The first is that the White students really enjoyed it. They said it was cool; they had a good time; they liked the house; and everyone was really nice to them. I was glad they had a good time, but angry that they just didn't get it. However, it wasn't their fault. It was ours for thinking that in one exercise, for a few hours on one evening, we could even come close to replicating the experiences of people of color who work in those positions their entire lives. I already knew that, of course, but I realized it in a more powerful and painful way than ever before. In trying to increase understanding of our issues and our experiences, the one thing we Latinos, Blacks, Asians, and other people of color will never be able to do is to recreate those exact experiences for White people. There are no exercises in the world that can ever fully and truly pass on that understanding. That's why our homework assignment for the White students failed.

The second thing that I noticed is how entrenched racism and racial superiority is in all of us. Just like in the movie "White Man's Burden," when we flip the script and all of a sudden Whites are serving people of color, it seems and feels totally absurd, ridiculous, fake, not real. Something is definitely wrong with that picture. It's like looking at another world. But when you flip it back and we are again the servers and Whites are on top, all seems normal, real. In fact, it is real. It's how our world really is. It is our daily reality. But it's just as absurd and ridiculous as the flip side. The only difference is, we are use to things this way. Whites and non-Whites, we all know it, ignore it, accept it, and live with it. We have internalized this crazy, absurd thing called racism and racial oppression.

Abel
Spring 1995

I identify as Xicano or Latino (and hardly ever Hispanic, except when perhaps trying to build coalitions with other Latinos).

My mother is from the Caribbean coast of Nicaragua and my father in Mexican. Since most of my mother's family was killed in the civil war in Nicaragua she was orphaned. Because I do not have a big sense of community from that side of my heritage, I identify more closely with my Mexican heritage. I emphasize that my mother is from the Caribbean coast because she is "negra," dark complexion, with definite African roots. While no one will ever say she has "bad hair," you can tell by her facial features the rich heritage and the past that she never wants to talk about.

My earliest memory of becoming aware of race was in elementary school. Like many of the kids from the Spanish speaking Barrio, the Mission district, I was bused out from my neighborhood under a court ordered consent decree. I was bused over to the other side of town to a predominantly Black school that was nestled between the central freeway and a housing project, both of which no longer exist today. While, the predominantly Black neighborhood has changed due to gentrification, my memories are very vivid. I always thought I was different because most of the kids that were brown like me were relegated to Room 22, a makeshift damp classroom in the basement of the school.

As I would pass by the classroom on my way to lunch, I would take a peek into a different world, a world in which I felt I belonged. But the teachers thought that "I spoke English pretty well," so there was no need for me to be in a bilingual education program. "We don't want to confuse him with another language," they explained to my mother as she smiled in total deference to my teachers. "You should learn English mijo, Ella es la maestra, ella sabe lo que es mejor," my mother would say. During recess, I would try to play with the other kids but they insisted on playing soccer instead of basketball or kickball like everyone else. The division line in the playground had already been drawn. Which side would I choose? Play with the native English speakers, or the English learners? Why must I choose? I understand both? Why I can't I play with both?

My best friend in elementary was Cory Johnson, the kid who was ostracized because he didn't celebrate any birthdays or holidays because he was a Jehovah's Witness. I didn't really know what that meant back then; I just thought he was smart, although I never knew why and never asked him why he did not even say the pledge of allegiance. Anyhow, as I was trying to negotiate my issues with difference I asked my friend Cory why he always drank chocolate milk. "I can't drink white milk because, mama says white milk is for White people and I am not white so I drink chocolate milk 'cause it looks like me." "My mom never told me that," I replied in disbelief. In an effort to try to come to terms with the politics of drinking milk, I felt that the milk I was drinking from the little orange carton did not look like me either. "Hey Cory!," I asked, "let me have some of you milk." I proceeded to mix my remaining milk with some of Cory's milk in an effort to find my color. I was not quite as dark as Cory was yet I was not as white as my milk. Finally I found the perfect combination, and I quickly showed my milk to Cory as I matched up to my skin to let him know that I found my shade that was not quite Cory's chocolate milk but not quite white as my regular ol' milk.

As I look back I laugh at these early negotiations with race, but I am reminded that even in today's race discussions, they seem to be debated in a duality of Black and White and everything else—yellow, brown, red—often times isn't even reflected in the discussions. The issues are way too complex to be diluted into a simple dichotomy as they often are in the media.

Although I had the opportunity to attend a prestigious East Coast school, the biggest factor in my choosing Cal was money and proximity to family. I was lucky in a sense. I was part of one of the first Incentive Awards Scholars cohorts, which awarded a four-year scholarship to students who had overcome adversity and demonstrated leadership and academic promise. My adversity was dealing with an abusive and alcoholic father and dealing with violent murders of my cousins who were shot in drive by shootings—one week after the other. There was no way I could leave my family and go across the country.

My experience at Cal was ideal for me. Ethnically, I think that my closest friends were all Latino, especially in the first year. I couldn't believe that there were so many other people who looked like me that had similar experiences. Wow, I thought, we've reached a critical mass of sorts. No longer would I be the only smart Latino or person of color in my classes the way it was in my high school honors and AP classes.

After the first year when I felt secure with myself, my group of friends started to mix up racially and ethnically. No longer did I just surround myself with people who looked like me. When I was a teenager, I was ashamed of being Mexican because I thought that was synonymous with Cholo or gangbanger. Everywhere I looked in my neighborhood, I didn't know one person who went to college. At one point I just conceded that college was for people who were White and rich. That was not me.

I had a few painful moments in the Ethnic Studies class, moments of anger and straight out ignorance. One day, a few of my White classmates and I were assigned to have an exchange or do something that I wouldn't normally do. One of the local pubs near campus is notoriously know for being the "frat boy" hangout. Well, it will be a good way to challenge myself and to learn to put myself in an uncomfortable situation. I just didn't know how uncomfortable. Seth and Megan invited me to Raleigh's. I told them I'd meet them at the bar. As soon as I walked in and handed the doorman my coat, I felt like the music stopped and the entire (predominantly White) clientele paused and all eyes were on me. "Oh my God," I thought. "I look that different?" Finally, I saw the warm and familiar faces of my classmates and quickly explained to them what I had just experienced. "Don't worry about it. It's just your imagination," they told me. "Look no one cares what you look like. Just have a beer and have a good time," pleaded Megan.

"Yeah, you're right, maybe it's just me," I thought. We started talking and I relaxed. A few minutes later a friend of Seth's comes over to the table and looks me up and down and then asks Seth, "Is this guy with you? What is he doing here? Are you practicing Spanish or something?" At that moment I didn't know whether I should hit the jerk or if I should leave or what. Seth began to apologize for his inebriated friend. At that moment I looked at Seth and Megan and said, " You see, I knew I wasn't full of shit." It pissed me off that this guy found it impossible that his White friends could be friends with or even just hang out with a Mexican. "Fuck those White frat boys," I thought, as I walked out of the bar with balled up fists and tears of anger in my eyes.

Because I was able to finally come to terms with and to be proud of my heritage, I was able to see the beauty and similarities in other peoples. By the time I graduated I can honestly say that my friends represented every shade and hue of the rainbow as well as every level and income bracket. I had a friend at Cal whose family couldn't afford spaghetti sauce so they would use ketchup as a substitute and a friend who owned a helicopter for fun.

Asian Americans

"I have been accused on countless occasions…that I have 'sold out my race and culture' because I do not speak Chinese…or do not join Chinese student organizations. My general attitude has always been that I am American…I am identifying that I am not Chinese but rather Chinese American."

—Richard, Fall 1998

Why I get angry

you ask me to talk about *Asian Americans*
one person representing the lives of
a diverse, fragmented, heterogeneous group
there isn't one type of *Asian American*
yet sometimes I feel like I'm being
lumped under very narrow, one-dimensional
stereotypes
I live in the library and have no social life nerd,
don't mess with me 'cause I'm best friends with
Bruce Lee ninja
gun-toting gang banging no respect
for American laws gangster,
I've come to take your jobs and live off welfare
illegal immigrant,
no speakee english fob,
I know exotic sexual techniques suzy wong
prostitute,

you can treat me like shit but I won't
complain passive sucker,
Harvard educated business suit clad
Mercedes Benz driving CEO

And we all look the same, right?
our *"Oriental"*
features
slanty-eyed, yellow skinned, straight black hair,
too short to pack your ass in basketball

no matter how wrong, how insulting
those images are, we never
raise our voices,
never demand
the truth,
never attempt to say
"No, you're WRONG. YOU
don't know me and the sad thing is,
you never tried."

Because to correct those misconceptions,
And bring the truth to the surface…
That would be borderline sacrilege
Asians don't argue…WRONG

I'm not your typical Asian…

I refuse to be ghettoized and categorized
I'm not going to give you the benefit
of assuming what kind of person
I am
I will fight all of your labels

I don't know how to turn on a computer
And don't ask me how to find the
derivative of sec x
       no, I'm not Chinese, Japanese, Korean, or Vietnamese
that's Pilipino with a "P" okay?
       why don't I answer to "Oriental"?
do you respond to nigger? cracker?
whitey? hispanic? wetback?
       you speak English real good
that's *really well*
       what's your nationality?
must I drape myself in an american flag
and eternally
hum the Star Spangled Banner
before
you recognize   I'm an american citizen
       gee, was the boat ride long or what?
boat ride? 18 of my nearly 20 years
of existence have been lived here in
america the beautiful
oh yeah, ***I flew***
       there are so many of your kind here at Cal
my kind? My kind what?
you know, Asians…
I'm second generation Pilipino American
get it straight

—***Chellyn***, *Fall 1993*

Richard
Fall 1998

The Tung family is originally from the Fu Zhou province of China; however, my father spent a portion of his childhood in Shanghai before the Communist Revolution. I can relate little about my family prior to this time, other than we had come from an upper-middle class of academics and bureaucrats. In my limited understanding of the social strata of the time, the class structure can be generally simplified into three groups: peasantry (lower class), academics and bureaucrats (middle class), and the imperial and elite landowners (upper class). My father was only a young boy at the time of the Communist Revolution, but recalls having to permanently expatriate to Taiwan during this time; however, his family had its primary residence in China.

This was a pivotal time in my family's history, as the political environment of the time robbed us, as it did others, of the ability to fully preserve our familial heritage. When I asked my father and grandparents about their ordeals during this time, they provided few answers to my questions, other than my father explaining that we had to abandon our home in China and much of our familial possessions along with it. At the time, my grandfather and family were already residing temporarily in Taiwan, but when the Communist Revolution took place, they found themselves unable to return. If you can imagine, it was almost as if you were on a family summer vacation in Mexico when suddenly your passports are no good and you can't get back across the border to go home because the Marines have moved into your house and have decided they like it enough to stay for a really long time. So basically, my family was stuck in Taiwan, left only with what they had packed for a temporary stay.

This was only a prelude to the even more perfidious circumstances of the political atmosphere in Taiwan. Once settled in Taiwan, my grandfather was now under suspicion of being a

Communist sympathizer by the Chinese Nationalists. He was a bit of a socialite and had many ties, so the danger of political suspicion was very real. Martial law was in effect at this time and secret police making unwarranted raids and arrests was common. This is precisely what happened to my grandfather when my father was no more than 6 years old. The police knocked on the door at 3:00 am, arrested my grandfather, and questioned my 6-year-old father about what his father spoke about and the people he spoke to. My father's most vivid recollection of the ordeal was that police came in and questioned him in an almost interrogation-like style about a book they found in the home, *Tom Sawyer*. The police believed the book to be written by Karl Marx and couldn't quite understand that it was not Marx who wrote the book, but Mark Twain. The police kept asking my father, "Who's book is this?" hoping to slate my grandfather as being an avid reader of Karl Marx. My father, being only six at the time, simply said, "It's mine!" After all, it was his book.

My grandfather was subsequently imprisoned for a term slightly longer than a year, after which time he was returned to his family and kept under regular surveillance for several years to follow. The reasons for his imprisonment are still unclear to me; however my understanding is that he narrowly escaped execution because he happened to be an acquaintance of the presiding judge of his case, who summarily acquitted him of any crime. (Legal due process was virtually non-existent at this time and executions were very common. If you were found guilty of a crime, you seldom received any opportunity to appeal—they simply executed you.)

The reason I relate these events is that they account for the general mentality my grandparents and parents adopted when emigrating to the United States: America was going to be their new home. My grandfather, being a more progressive thinker, had always had a great interest in western culture, which was subsequently instilled in my father. This is why it was important that my parents be educated in America and to eventually settle here.

Although my parents would disagree, I believe this had had a deep effect on my own perception of our place in Chinese culture. In a way, my family became the bastard children of Chinese culture: displaced by Communists in the mainland as well as the Nationalists in Taiwan. Traditional heirlooms, photographs, and family possessions were all either reclaimed by the Communists or lost in the turmoil of time spent in Taiwan. And so, my family became much like many American families—expatriated foreigners who sought to replant roots and build anew. When you ask my parents how they identify themselves, they will tell you that they are Chinese. But although they are Chinese, they also feel that they are now American and have raised American children. My father stepped on American soil in 1962 with a passport and no more wealth than the prospect of his youth and industry. At this time, he realized the daunting task ahead of him—the task which we continue to struggle against: gaining equal acceptance and prosperity in a country in which we are a minority and disadvantaged by the cultural gap created by the perception that "we just got here."

My relationship with my parents has always been a "no frills" sort of relationship—my brother and I were raised on practicality and the notion that there is always a solution to every problem and that emotions are only well spent when sharing with loved-ones. All other matters can be dealt with in a dispassionate and methodical manner. Our family unit is small. Our communications with the few extended family members we have are infrequent, and reunions are seldom. Realistically, my brother and I have always considered "our family" my father, mother, my brother and myself.

As I was growing up, both my parents always impressed upon me the importance of academic excellence. When my parents settled here in the sixties, student scholarships were essentially the only means of getting a visa, so education became the all-important tool an immigrant needed to be successful in America. My father, himself, had received his Ph.D. in solid-state physics, and my mother did her graduate studies in history, so higher education was always a primary goal. To that end, my brother and I were raised with a competitive "rough edge," where we were not allowed to do poorly on an exam or let some classmate outperform us in a subject. Dinner conversations were focused on current events and/or politics; mandatory supplemental reading reinforced class curriculum; and daily "lessons" in self-reliance and independent thinking taught us to be competitive. One circumstance that will always remind me of my parents' toughness was when my mother taught me to read a map. I was 10. She had my father drop us off three miles from home in the middle of Irvine suburbia with a map of town. She said, "Here's a map. You tell me where we are and I'm going to follow you home." It took me three hours to find our way home out of the suburban maze of cul de sacs and looped communities. Every so often during this ordeal, I would ask my mother if we were in the right place and received no more validation than, "I don't know—you tell me." It sure felt like a lot of pressure at the time, considering the day was quickly turning to night and my only experience with city streets prior to this point was viewed from the back seat of a car. In retrospect, I think it was strange growing up with parents who occasionally adopted the "figure it out for yourself" method of teaching, but I think I've grown to appreciate their method since.

Mastery of the English language was always an interesting issue, as my parents insisted that being able to communicate on the same elevated intellectual level as our white counterparts was essential to becoming successful in America. The only problem was that they weren't ideal role models for speaking English. This is not to say that they lacked command of the English language. They frequently used advanced vocabulary but simply had a difficult time with grammar and pronunciation. This was often a tender issue for my parents because they believed in good presentation and communication skills being a valuable mode for gaining acceptance in American culture as minorities. Basically if you were smart, tough, and could communicate on the same level as those who held power in society, you had a likelier chance of breaking the glass ceiling for yourself.

Throughout my primary education, most of our Orange County community consisted of middle-class white families. My brother and I learned to live with the constant burden of having to dispel Asian stereotypes about Kung Fu and slanted eyes. I recall times when this bothered me a little, but children are frequently color-blind and injuries quickly heal and are as easily forgotten. For the most part, my classmates throughout elementary school considered me an equal, and my race never affected my ability to make friends. The fact is I had a lot of friends growing up, and I don't recall race ever being an issue with my peers. I think I was more concerned with particular misunderstandings adults made of me during this time. In third grade, I recall a Taiwanese student joined our class, but he was utterly hopeless in speaking English. Being the only other student of Asian extraction in the class, my teacher asked if I could translate the class instructions for him. I would have been more than willing to oblige had I any command of the Chinese language; however, I only spoke English. I felt a bit awkward explaining to my teacher that I had not the foggiest notion how to communicate with this foreigner. Looking back on that experience, I considered it a harmless misunderstanding but found it unfortunately unjust that people would leap to the conclusion that my yellow skin, straight black hair, and almond shaped eyes automatically predetermined that I could probably speak Chinese. This prejudice was and still is something that Italian Americans, German Americans, and even African Americans will encounter less because they "look" American, and there is an automatic expectation that they speak English. Asian Americans and Chicanos, however, are sometimes expected to first speak Chinese or Spanish before speaking English because the perception is that we are only recent immigrants to this country.

To me, there is an important distinction to make here. There is a difference between natively born Asian Americans and Asian Americans like my parents who are expatriated from their country of birth. I have been accused on countless occasions throughout secondary and collegiate education that I have "sold out my race and culture" because I don't speak Chinese, because I don't care to celebrate Chinese New Year, or because I don't join Chinese Student organizations. My general attitude has always been that I am American. Modifying this descriptor with Asian American only allows others to place an immediate prejudice, however unwitting and innocent as it may be, upon their perception of me. This is not to say that I am shirking my heritage or denying the color of my skin. Instead, I am identifying that I am not Chinese but rather Chinese American—just as Italian Americans, German Americans, Russian Americans, African Americans and Mexican Americans do. The common denominator is that we are all American. Everyone has his/her own definition of heritage and culture, so I find it ultimately important that I not be identified with a culture that has closer ties to Chinese history than I have. I don't speak Chinese, I've never stepped foot on Chinese soil, and I don't eat every meal with a pair of chopsticks and a bowl of rice. I do, however, occasionally eat traditional Chinese cuisine, just as I eat European or even Mediterranean cuisine. The great luxury we have as Americans is that we *can* appreciate multiple cultures—this, in my opinion, is what comprises an American culture.

My friends throughout elementary school tended to be White, as a White population in general dominated the demographics of Irvine. The next most common ethnic group was the Asian American community, which proliferated considerably shortly after I started junior high school. The difficult aspect of my growth at this time is that I began to notice ethnicities drawing away from each other and Balkanizing into different ethnic "clumps." By the time I hit high school, I found refuge in the Honors student population, which was expectedly diverse in ethnic makeup. As an honors student, I felt ethnic barriers, slightly mitigated by the fact that we all strove to excel in academics and land ourselves at some prestigious educational institution after high school.

An odd encounter I consider worth noting is a comment one of my instructors made to me in a class discussion regarding the oppression of minorities in the Irvine community. I felt the discussion had been too focused on African Americans and Latino Americans and so I was attempting to posit that Chinese Americans, too, were a minority that had experienced different forms of prejudice. My instructor said, "Oh, come on, Richard. The Asians in Irvine are essentially White. You've all grown up in privileged homes with intelligent parents and stable sources of income." I remember feeling falsely accused at the time and trying to palm myself off as the "oppressed minority." Now, looking back, I understand my instructor's point but still have contentious feelings as to whether I totally agree with her statement. I think I agree that I've lived in a sheltered and privileged community, but I also feel she was a little myopic about her own evaluation of the Chinese American culture in Irvine. She understood it, all right—the Chinese American students in our honors classes weren't all expatriated foreigners who had to learn English from scratch but much like myself—raised as Americans. But she seemed so caught up in having identified us as different from other Asian immigrants that she automatically pigeon-holed us once again by making the generalization that we were just like white students. It's difficult to categorize people by race when there is such diversity within any given race.

This brings me to my Berkeley years and the reason I found myself in the seminar. My unpopular ethnic opinions landed me in the Berkeley Fraternity community, where I convinced enough of the Greek community that I would be a good leader for the Interfraternity Council. In time, I became the Interfraternity Vice President of Recruitment and subsequently President of the governing organization. This brought me much pleasure, as it provided me, for the first time, an environment in which I could share my social beliefs with other students who cared as much (or as little) about ethnicity as I did. In case this isn't making much sense, the Berkeley Greek community is very much atypical of other schools in that it is a very accurate ethnic cross-section of the Berkeley student population overall. Many of the individual chapters do not consist of any fewer than three ethnicities, with no particular weight towards one. In my own chapter, we had more than ten distinct ethnicities, and none maintained a majority of the overall membership. This was fascinating to me because we cared very little from which ethnic or socio-economic background new members came—rather, we were bound purely by common interest, whether it was sports, music, areas of study or even label of beer. Imagine a Syrian American drinking beer and belching with Persian Jewish-, Sri Lankan-, Asian-, Chicano- and White American fraternity brothers? —That's literally what we had. In my opinion, the Greek community at Cal was the one most diverse and largest student organization on campus, because anyone could join. It was cheaper than living in the dorms, and it encouraged active participation in campus events of all kind. I have no doubt that many people outside the Greek community would disagree, but having had an intimate association in this organization, I believe this to be true. For once, I wasn't being identified by race. I still contend that the Greek community provides just as much education as the academic side of Berkeley because it's a value-based education. This environment helped me identify what I really find valuable in my life: family, friendship, loyalty and integrity.

So when I was invited to participate in his class, I first felt privileged to have been invited and then looked forward to taking part in the many discussions that were to be generated. I think my first encounters with the other students had been very positive. Everyone seemed very open-minded and friendly, which helped me become very open. But as discussions progressed, I found myself very much surprised. Surprised at the ordeals others had experienced; surprised that the perspectives I had assumed they would take were contrary to my assumptions. No matter how open-minded you think you are, assumptions and prejudices seem to always sneak their way into your own perception and affect your judgment. I found these surprises to be refreshing because they helped me look back at myself and re-evaluate my own perspectives on other people—not based upon their race or ethnicity but rather their individual experiences. This requires a great deal of attention and concentration; it's very easy to become complacent and judge people generally when you need to be observing individually. Just like my family's experiences and ordeals, race and ethnicity were for the most part incidental. But herein lie many of my criticisms of the accounts that took place in our class discussions.

Many of the stories told in discussion were impressive: everyone seemed to have overcome some hardship or dealt with some difficult ordeal that ultimately made them stronger characters. I had a great deal of respect for my peers, and felt I grew to empathize with them more. However, there were points in our discussions where it seemed there emerged a common mantra: "You don't understand what we've been through...you say you understand and you say you're listening, but you don't really understand and you aren't really listening." I noticed this attitude on several different occasions, many of which resulted in one or more students breaking down into tears. As callous as this may seem, and as empathetic I still believe myself to be, I simply took the attitude, "Well if you don't think I'm really listening and you don't think I really understand, then fine—I won't listen to you and I won't care about what you've endured." I found this reaction unsettling because it occurred to me that if you really want people to empathize with you and listen to your concerns, you also have to be open enough to let them do so. Closing oneself off and holding onto hardship like some badge of honor does little if anything to help others understand you; rather, it makes others antagonistic, defensive and equally closed off. I think some of my classmates who shared this view felt rejected. I recall one incident where four classmates burst into tears in one class sitting—one over the hardship he had suffered, one because she felt nobody was listening, and the other two because they felt blamed and denied the chance to understand. I related most to the latter two. We had been so open and honest, and when we wanted most to empathize with our colleagues, we were prohibited to do so because our ordeals didn't happen to be as egregiously traumatic or incapacitating as our counterparts'.

I recall at these moments that my temperance faltered, and I found myself gesticulating about how parading around campus and banding together in ethnic cliques would never help the minority cause. I found myself saying to myself: "these people should quit their complaining and concentrate on actionable steps in improving themselves. Everyone has problems and everyone has experienced hardship, but having character means that you don't sit and cry about how you'd been wronged by society—having character means you deal with each problem individually and practically." Looking back, these thoughts are hard words to live by, but I still believe the idea is correct. Drawing upon my own upbringing and upon what I know my class colleagues to be capable of, I believe that each participant is extremely strong in his/her own way but just like anybody else, including myself, it is easier to point the finger and transfer blame elsewhere. Blame is a funny thing when you deal with ethnic and racial issues—you end up over-generalizing and placing blame on groups as opposed to individuals. The problem with placing blame on groups is that you invariably end up blaming individuals who do not necessarily deserve the blame. The reaction is a self-perpetuating cycle of retribution, contention, distrust and antagonism.

Sometimes things are the way they are for that reason alone, but it behooves us all individually to approach each hardship without malice but with a heuristic practicality that may offer solutions. One of the common reactions I noticed in class was one in which a White colleague would say to one of our minority colleagues something to the effect of—"You're blaming us for being more privileged than you but I've never done anything to wrong your culture." I recall this distinctly because I noticed her use of the word "us" and this disturbed me. For some reason or another, our discussion moved from being a group of intelligent individuals sharing individual experiences to a discussion caught up in an "us versus them" mentality. In situations like these, I feel the only way to bring contextual perspective back to the discussion is by being introspective and self-analytical to find out where communication had broken down. Once communication can be reestablished, reasonable practicality is restored, and problems can then be offered solutions.

There was frequently a double standard unwittingly set by many of the participants in the class, too. Admittedly, I caught myself guilty of that same double standard, but I think this was part of everyone's learning experience, if you can catch yourself or allow others to catch you. At one point, I was being made to feel guilty for "denying my heritage." An African American classmate actually asserted her disgust at my "not acknowledging my own heritage." (Shortly prior to this, I had been accused of not listening to another classmate's comments, so I had become particularly both defensive and aggressive at the same time.) My only response was that if she had only been listening she would understand that I wasn't denying my heritage at all. In fact I was attempting to redefine my heritage to help my classmates better understand me. I'm still not very good at responding to people who foist their values and beliefs on me. In this particular situation, this classmate seemed to be projecting her own belief in how to value one's own culture onto me, whether or not I agreed. This was interesting because she wasn't listening to me, and I wasn't listening to her.

At the time I found this discussion extremely disconcerting; we were simply not communicating. I still do not think she understood me and I think she will continue to harbor feelings of disgust for me. But in retrospect, being able to recognize that we weren't listening to each other has helped me in subsequent conflicts in other aspects of my personal life. Just because somebody doesn't share the same beliefs and values doesn't mean you don't listen to them. In almost all cases, you need to listen more carefully because the people you meet will always have different beliefs and values. And you don't even have to agree with those values. You just have to respect that they have different values. The sooner this happens, the better you will understand that person and the better your communications will be. This is hard to learn because I think people are innately self-interested, and it's easy to think what you feel and ignore other perspectives. I think my parents were right—if you want to get ahead in America, you need to be able to communicate. They just never told me how difficult it is to learn to communicate. You have to learn all the time with everyone you meet.

I'm not really quite sure what to say about the quality of my relationships with people of other ethnicities. I guess I'm lucky— I live in San Francisco, where diversity is a fact of life and there isn't much tolerance for intolerance. I try my best to ignore ethnicity and concentrate on personal merits, but despite my efforts, I confess most of my friends and associates are still either white or Asian in ethnic makeup. I'm not sure how it happened that way, but I'd be artificial if I tried too hard to make sure I mixed in a couple of extra colors. The simple fact of the matter is people in the city are more driven by the almighty dollar and dot.com IPOs than they are by the color of your skin. That's why friends are so important. I'm happy to say that many of my best friends from school are from different ethnic backgrounds and are all willing to share their different cultures with one another. But this fact really shouldn't matter. They're not my friends necessarily because of their ethnicity; they're my friends because we have common and different interests and common and different experiences. So what is the quality of my relationships with people of other ethnic groups? I guess I'd say they're pretty good, since I do have friends from so many different ethnic groups. But if chance would have it that they were all Black, all White, or all Yellow, I don't think my answer would be any different. They would just be different people—not ethnicities.

Jidan
Spring 1996

My name means Red/Fiery Determination. I am the first daughter, born in 1975 after the high point of the Third World strike, to two first generation Chinese UC Berkeley grads. Both my parents were very active in the Third World strike, the Asian American Studies Movement, and community organizing/service efforts in San Francisco Chinatown. I grew up with movies about Turkish resistance, Del Norte, Rosa Luxembourg, Eyes on the Prize (the Civil Rights Movement), the Chinese Revolution, and Palestine. The only non-book present my father ever gave me was a red ribbon from the South African Divestment movement at Cal. By the age of twelve, I knew in my heart the beauty and courage that heroes around the world displayed when they stood up against inequity—and many of them were not much older than me.

From the stories that circled around me and the people I came into contact with while growing up, I appreciated the many privileges I had as a child who had enough to eat and a place to stay the night. In junior high, I took part in community organizing efforts in some of the "worst" most infamous public housing complexes in the Bay Area, including Sunnydale, Potrero Hill and Acorn. My younger sister and I helped take over abandoned public housing units to house the homeless. We went to homeless shelters to recruit homeless people to stay in the newly opened up units. We slept there together in the day and stayed up all night on watch for the police. We ate food, not bombs, for dinner and showered periodically at different people's houses.

Many "conscious" folks with middle class or wealthier backgrounds want to disown their privileges. I have seen enough to know that everyone deserves a nice place to live—and if one happens to have a nice place, why be defensive or ashamed of it? My mother used to work at Safeway, and I would be damned to tell her that she was "selling out" when she wanted to get a doctor's degree, own her home, and have a view. Some "conscious" people at Cal use the word "bougie" (short for bourgeoisie) to describe negative things that they feel characterize the middle class. For instance, if they would visit a nice house, they would say, "this is a bougie place" to hint that this is not the place a "down" person would live. These kinds of people glorify living in the ghetto and think that there is something cool about not having money. There is nothing cool about not having a pencil to do your homework or enough money to get on the bus to go to school. I like to live in a place where I can feel safe to walk around at night. I appreciate privileges like that. More than that, I am proud to share what I have with others.

Although I grew up conscious of race, class, and gender inequity, I absorbed many forms of self-hate that I became aware of and battled in college. Many times I struggled through it in Stiles' class. As I looked back on my junior high and high school experience, I realized that I was ignorant of the struggles of many new Asian Pacific Islander immigrants. When I was little, I remembered being ashamed of my Chinese-speaking grandma when she came to my school and I had also bought into stereotypes about Korean people. I rejected things considered "girly" and embraced "maleness" as a way to "empower" myself. I called other girls sluts and hoes, and felt superior over other Asian students at my school because I was American born.

In high school, I began to deal with my racial self-hatred. I think my mother and father assumed that I would derive Asian pride from them. However, in growing up, I happened to associate more with African Americans and did not know a lot about

Asian Pacific American history because there was very little available in terms of cultural education for Asian Pacific Islander American (API) students. I joined the Black Student Union (BSU) when I first got to high school because I had some African American studies classes. Although I valued BSU, I knew that it did not deal with issues that were specific to my ethnicity.

In the tenth grade, one of the most important things in my life happened. After an arrest, I was referred to the East Bay Asian Youth Center—a non-profit agency that served API students at risk. Wow! What a revelation to participate in Asian Pacific summer school! I got involved in the Asian Pacific Student Union at my school and found a place where I could lead peers in addressing the issues we faced as API students. I found a place where my history and family were recognized–in essence, I found a place to exist.

After high school, I went to UC Berkeley. Being local gave me a huge opportunity to engage college students in work with the community. I participated in Asian Pacific empowerment activities as well as coalition building with other ethnically based student groups. In my college sophomore and junior years, my sister and I started a mentorship for API students from Oakland. Because we operated "from scratch"—without knowledge of mentoring best practices—I felt it was important for me to find out about other mentoring models. Thus, I got involved in Stiles, which is the most well known mentorship provider at UC Berkeley, as a mentor and then as a mentorship coordinator.

After some persistence on the part of the instructor, I also took the class. It turned out to be an important decision because the class gave me an opportunity to get to know leaders from other ethnic communities and renew my feelings towards multi-cultural collaboration. At first, I was weary to use parts of my packed schedule to do what seemed to be an extra task with no real-world application. I also was weary of participating in multi-cultural discussions because I often would have to take the role of dispelling deep-seated myths about Asian people. As many people of color have said before, when so many of "our own" are uneducated about us—why spend precious time educating "others" about us? That, unfortunately, is sometimes how I feel about educating "others" about Asian Pacific Islanders.

The interaction in the class was not like I had expected. Students were open about hearing other opinions and sharing theirs. We agreed to disagree. I realized that many organizers on campus build an insular world where large differences of opinion on issues of race, class, and gender do not exist. None of my friends would say that welfare is bad, or that they supported Prop.187, or that racism does not exist. All of a sudden, I was put into contact with people who were on the opposite political spectrum, and it forced me to really think through how to argue my side as well as recognize how difficult it is to communicate with people who come from completely different life experiences.

Steven
Spring 1993

I think to my parents, with their traditional Korean ways, college was not only a necessity, but also a symbol of superiority. The "better" the school (or more accurately, the more notoriety the school had), the "better" my parents felt about themselves. You see, I grew up in a value system where every child was expected to attend college. Thus, for my parents' generation, the "measuring stick" was based on what colleges your kids got into. If I attended a university that could be recognized by almost anyone in the world, then, had I not only done my duty as a son to attend college and exceeded expectations by making my parents look good (or save "face") in front of others. There is an added bonus to this. It follows that since the son had been raised "right"—that is, he has performed his duty—the parents earned the right to be "superior" to other parents. And being "superior" to others was what it was all about.

Although I was lucky in that my parents never shared these views explicitly, other parents (i.e. my aunts and uncles and family friends) have always compared my academic success to other children. This quiet competition started in kindergarten. I remember my mom trying to get a list of the "Top 30 Kindergartens in Seoul" when it was my time. She never told me what it was for, but I remember Mom being really happy when I won the lottery to attend a particular kindergarten. You may think that this sort of stuff happens in a far way land in some distant past, but even to this day, major Korean-Americans newspapers publish the academic rankings of elementary, junior, and senior high schools in all metropolitan cities in the United States! Early on, I knew that adults wanted me to succeed so that they could "show off" or, more accurately, shut the rest of the competition up. It is ironic how most Korean parents teach their children to be humble and to fit in with the rest, while emphasizing (in the privacy of their homes) that one must outdo others; that there is nothing more shameful than not succeeding in school; that a "B" is not a grade that is acceptable—let alone a "C."

Despite these social pressures, I wanted to go to college for a different reason. I figured I could buy and read any textbook I wanted. I didn't need to go to college for the "book knowledge." To me, college was a place to meet new people and gain new ideas. It was also an opportunity for me to try the things that I was not allowed to do in high school. I still believe that the most important thing you can learn from college is how to interact with other people rather than gaining "technical knowledge." The value of attending class is in the human interaction with your professors, the teaching assistants and the fellow students. No matter which career I choose, the technical knowledge I have learned in college will soon be outdated, but one constant thing is that I will be interacting with other people. Some will like me. Others will not. And just in case I am ever stuck with a boss that does not like me, I wanted to learn how to interact with other people positively. Thus, I wanted to attend a college that provided the right opportunity and the surroundings to enrich my social experience rather than a college that provided the "safe environment" that was nothing more than a continuation of my high school days.

After I decided to attend Cal, the word spread through the grapevine. I got calls from cousins and uncles that I didn't even know I had. It became evident that I had to go visit my Granduncle. Since the communists took my Granddad up to North Korea during the Korean War, my Granduncle took over as the head of the family. This entitled him to know everything about my family and to hold on to the family tree. So, I needed to go pay my respects. Whenever I visit him, my Granduncle always shows me the family tree. It consists of 120 volumes of family lineage that officially goes back 52 generations. (Unofficially, it goes back about 76 generations, but for practical purposes, we usually limit our discussions to the 52 generations). All of my ancestors are recorded in these books and are neatly displayed along the entire wall of my Granduncles' room. My immediate family's names are entered in the last volume. Towards the last pages of the last volume, my dad's name appears. Next to it is my mother's. Below is my name with a space left open for my future wife. And my younger brother's name and a space reserved for his future wife is recorded below mine.

It wasn't until the summer of my sophomore year that I had a chance to visit my Granduncle in Korea. Like countless times before, he greeted me, offered me some tea, and showed me my entry in the book. But this time, it was different. Rather than getting the book himself, he had asked me to do it. So I reached for the book that had my name entered in it, turned to "my page" and found a new entry next to my name. No, it was not a name of a woman I am supposed to marry. It read: Steven: U.C. Berkeley.

There were no congratulations and no pleasantries. Instead, my Granduncle said, "Why didn't you go to Ha Ba D (Harvard)? I had a difficult time finding out the spelling of some obscure school that no one knows." As I looked up, his eyes were smiling. He always had a way of down playing some big events in life. I thanked him for his troubles, offered him some more tea and discussed what I was going to study.

It didn't take long before the conversation changed. As the first-born son, I had always been treated differently. I think since my birth, people have always told me that I was the "first born son" as if that entitled me to everything. I was given a special place to sit whenever the family (that is all 50 or so of them) got together. I was "prepped" in how to conduct myself. Even as a child, I had a personal servant and access to privileged information about my family that no one else (including my mother) knew about—because I needed to know this critical information to make the "right" decisions in the future. Now that I have gotten into a college, it was time for me to get the complete story about all the members of my family.

Growing up, I would often wonder why some of my uncles were treated differently. For example, during some ceremonies older men would usually be seated at the head of the tables. But some of my uncles were not seated according to the convention. One uncle would offer me the master bedroom to sleep in while he and his wife would retire to the "guest bedroom" whenever I visited them. Little things like these discrepancies would baffle me. Now that I have become of age, everything was revealed to me. No one, except the current and the future "heads" of the family (i.e. my father, Granduncle, and I) were allowed to listen during this conversation. My Granduncle with stern, deep coughs dismissed the ladies, who would usually help with the serving of the tea and the rest of the treats. They discreetly asked my brother to leave the room with them.

The conversation took a few hours. Afterwards, I knew almost more than what I care to know about my family. All of my questions were answered. Unfortunately, they are things that I cannot share with anyone. My father had asked me to take them with me to my grave. Without getting into the specifics, words like concubine, religious differences, political persecutions, disputes over the land, and family wars were mentioned. So now, I have the burden of making decisions about my family that no one else would truly understand. I also have to deal with the fact that I will not be able to share some of my most intimate thoughts with anyone. Growing up, my younger brother would get jealous of my getting all the attention. A few years ago, after seeing all the responsibilities that I have to deal with, he jokingly told me that he never wants to be me, and that his first child would be a "second son."

But there are privileges to being the patriarch. My grandpa (on my mother's side) excelled at showing his class distinction as a Yang Ban (i.e. High Class) who owned most of the farmland in the village. I think it is because he had lived in a time where class distinctions were not only tolerated, but also flaunted. When I was three, I had an opportunity to live with him. The first thing my grandpa did was to get me a personal servant. From what my mom tells me, I was a cruel "master." One winter night, (it was about 3 in the morning) I was shaken by the wind, and wanted to sleep with my mom. Rather than telling me "no," my mom had made a comment that my hands were dirty and that they smelled. Instead of going back to sleep, I called for my servant. I dragged him out of bed at 3 in the morning, got him to go down to the well, heat up the freezing water, and bring it to my room so that I can wash my hands. At three, I really did not comprehend that I was being mean. Rather, I thought that this was a natural way for me to behave because my grandfather told me in the morning that I had done the "right thing."

At the farm, my grandfather always took his meals by himself. He was the first one to be served—getting all the choice meats and vegetables. Then, the rest of the "men" (which included my father, my uncles, my younger brother, and myself) ate what was left over from my grandfather's meal. When the "men" were done with our meal, the ladies had what was left over in the kitchen. I never actually saw them eating. I just knew that they were in the kitchen. Moving back to Seoul changed that; that is, without my grandparents, there was no one to enforce the old ways to us, and we had no servants. From then on, I ate my meals prepared by my mom with her sitting by my side at the table.

Moving to America, some of our traditional Korean values had to be changed. The sexist and class distinctions were no longer practiced in my family but the "racial aspect" still remained. When I came to Diamond Bar, I did not speak any English. Being one of the first non-American children to attend their school, the folks at the elementary school did their best and placed me in a class of deaf children. Here, I learned sign language faster than I learned English. Needless to say, I became a subject of constant ridicule at recess time. This fueled my bitter sentiment towards some of my classmates, and things soon escalated into fights. I was mostly fighting other minority students. My mom would always tell me to be careful of "Blacks," and that the "Mexicans" should not be my friends. My folks had never had any interactions with any other race besides Koreans. What little they knew about other races came from the old TV shows that only perpetuated the stereotypes. Naturally, I treated these kids coldly, and they reacted back. To make matters worse, I did not understand what they were saying so I perceived most of their behaviors as hostile.

High school changed all that. In my classes, I saw kids from other racial backgrounds that excelled in the subjects being taught had great athletic abilities, and were even decent human beings. I started making friends with all kinds of people because I needed to adjust my values in order for me to succeed in high school. At home, the stereotypical sentiment still remained, and I cringed every time my mom would say some derogatory remarks about a "non-White" person. I knew that these things were simply not true. I wanted to say something to my mom, but at the time, I didn't have the vocabulary to challenge her views. And challenging my parent's views was simply not done in my house.

Having mostly Caucasian friends does influence your behavior no matter how Korean you think you may be at home. I spoke Korean to my parents and all of my relatives, read Korean books and even watched Korean videos to maintain some of my heritage. But I was surrounded by my "American" friends when I was not home. Perhaps that is why I appeared "whitewashed" to some of my Asian associates. Most of the Korean students that I had met at Cal thought that I was either Japanese, or Chinese, and definitely "whitewashed"—in other words, not their own. I don't know why people think that I am not Korean. But I have recently found out that my family is not "100% Korean" as we would like to believe. I may get into some big trouble for this, but I think it needs to be said. You see, I found out that our family was actually from Manchuria, had mixed with some Mongolian blood and eventually settled in Korea. This is why we only discuss the family lineage up to the 52nd generations. Adding to the confusion, my grandmother's family can trace their lineage back to India, so I think it is only fitting that some of us appear "foreign." But most Koreans that I run into never express it like that—they usually say that "there is something not right" as if they can claim their Korean blood to be of a "pure blood."

I face this kind of racism and discrimination from all sides. To the racist Caucasians, I am not white enough. To the racist Koreans, I am not Korean enough. When I walk through the streets in Arizona, people stare at me because of my obvious Asian features. When I walk though the streets of Seoul, people still stare at me. At Yi Tae Won (which is a discount market place next to a U.S. military base) the merchants address me first in Japanese, then in English. It boggles their mind that I could be a part of them, let alone speak their language.

In the class, I met a group of wonderful people who changed my life forever. To be honest, all the academic classes that I attended at Cal (not to discredit some of my eloquently spoken Professors) are now big blurs of theories all blended into one massive, obscure thought called Psychology. But my experience at Stiles Hall, has never lost its distinctive place in my heart. It has taught me to reflect on my values, change, adept, and interact with human beings rather than being an ignoramus with my preconceived stereotypes.

Stiles Hall's Ethnic Studies class reminded me of an Encounter Group. It was a form of group therapy in which the participants actually have the autonomy to lead the topic of discussion rather than handing over that power to the therapist. There were a number of projects that I had to do for the class. One was to live for five days on five dollars. Living on a jar of peanut butter, taking only 5 scoops a day, I couldn't tell my friends why I couldn't join them for coffee (which cost couple of bucks a pop). And I surely could not go out to dinner—let alone a beer! Soon, I realized that most people think that you do not belong in the society (that there is something indeed very troubling and wrong with you) if you do not have money to spend. Just go to a restaurant with your friends without ordering anything and see it for yourself.

Another project was to visit a public place that a person of my racial background would usually not go. I attended a Catholic mass held by a Mexican priest. The entire congregation was Mexican. Most of the men wore their cowboy boots, hats, and huge belt buckles and stood dignified and proud. They looked at me wondering, "who is this guy?" But no one asked me to leave. No one stared with animosity. They quietly accepted my presence and welcomed me with warm smiles and even warmer handshakes. Sometimes, you do not need words to convey a positive sentiment to your fellow beings. They were just happy that I had chosen to come. They even offered me some lunch—and I could not refuse. I spent the afternoon using hand gestures and body language to tell these kind of people that I was doing this for a class. They were very receptive. One lady even complemented me on getting into Cal and asked me back. They were not the people that my mother had believed they were. In fact, they reminded me a lot of my own family and their ways.

One day, a classmate named Jose (who is a Native American) walked in with a "Cleveland Caucasians" baseball cap which started a whole discussion about the covert racism in our culture that we are all exposed to but do not think about. This particular class taught me that we sometimes do things out of ignorance and hope that everything will be forgiven—because we did not intend on offending someone. But I wonder if that hurts the victim any less.

Receiving racism and discrimination from ignorant people does not bother me anymore. I guess, over the years, I have managed to grow a tougher exterior. Actually, I think I have grown to understand other perspectives. The class forced me to do that. It broke down my stereotypes because you cannot stand in other people's shoes unless you take yours off first. From there, you discover that there are many commonalties amongst all people.

I work at MTV now. Working in the entertainment industry, I see some "freaky" people doing some "crazy" stuff. In dealing with the various perspectives that are in this business, I apply a lot of psychological theories that I learned in school. But most of the day, I use the skills that I have learned at Stiles Hall. They truly are the most useful skills that I learned in school.

Patty
Spring 1999

I sense resentment from other minority groups directed towards Asians—as if we have achieved success and acceptance, at the expense of others. So no, Asians certainly do not belong in the category of "underrepresented minority." Yet in American companies, how many Asian executives do you see? How many yellow faces in the state and federal legislature? How many times do you hear that a candidate is "courting the yellow vote?"

I feel, rather, that the difficulties Asian-Americans face are ones of acceptance as Americans. While African-Americans arguably face more overt and severe discrimination and stereotyping, they are for the most part, still considered "American." No matter what racial epithets are used, it would seem strange to hear "go back to where you came from" directed at Blacks.

Chanthip
Fall 1998

Diversity is something to be appreciated, but it doesn't just come. You have to search for it. You have to interact with other students. One of the hardest things to do is challenge your own experiences. However, in order to really grow and take advantage of the rare environment of this class, you have to be able to face your own fears and realize that you may not understand many things, but with every person you meet you may get a little closer.

African Americans

"I recently spoke to a Jewish girl who graduated with
my sister… She asked me didn't I just hate how
White and oppressive the whole environment was. I
had to tell her "No." I do not expect for White people
to be anything other than oppressive and White."
—Kerri, Spring 1998

Native Sons and Daughters of America:
This is the way Biggers are Born

Black tears fall on white fears
And they make gray, like the earth's clay, like those cold days
When slaves froze in quarters but their spirits burned in pain.

Black bodies fall like rain and the fact that little has changed makes
me ask,
Do my people die in vain?

I see reflections of Christ in black faces but
Police actions defame Gods name

Sirens sing songs of service but resonate with songs of suffering,
Sound-scapes are broken and serene street scenes violated

Crimson tears stain city streets
Where white cops see ethnic notions in the night

And white jeers hit black ears and nightmares replay during the day

Endless greed gives birth to the racial realities we live
And race notions bind the flitting spaces where souls meet

Race beats heavy on my heart and my heart beats heavy cause I'm running one
Fed from the ample bosom of Amaleikkka.

Only now realizing that its ideological nourishment poisoned my senses, I walk among the corrupted members of race's family and gaze at unfamiliar faces whose eyes house hatred within.

Liberation seems aloof and proof lies behind lies, and we cling to lies while lives go by
My history shows that violence is the strongest form of prose
For those who oppose those who oppress

The truth is suppressed and mis-education is impressed on young minds that find love difficult to express.

Courts become middle passages to
Prisons that provide public peace-of-mind and private profits combined

The fears black mothers feel consume children in the womb
And babies are birthed with shattered dreams and bluest eye complexes

Bloodstains paint portraits of reality exposing the fact that meritocracy is the propaganda of democracy, which is bought and sold as commodity commonly.

A people that put the hue in humanity are dehumanized and hast-
ily herded into hoods
So drugs can be introduced and minds induced into self-destruc-
tive sentiments; society finds its scapegoat

Politics speak in codes that translate into de-membered black
family ties

The souls of black folk speakeasy but give sound advice: "Stop
the trails of tears, know truth and live reality, don't let more Biggers
get born."

—*Cameron,* Spring 2000

Kerri
Spring 1998

Both sets of my grandparents were Black. Actually, my paternal
grandmother may have been half Native American—Cherokee
to be more specific. I am not totally sure how much Native American influence I have from that side of my family. What I think of
as strong Native American traits—long aquiline nose, long straight
and very thick hair, slightly slanted eyes—definitely come through
on both my sister and me, and even more so in my father's siblings.

One trait that has been passed on from my grandparents to
my mother and on to my sister and me is that when we are angry
we do not lash out, and we do not yell (at least initially). We simply
close off the rest of the world until we are able to reconcile within
ourselves what the problem is. I am not sure how much of a
function this is of being Black, but I do know that when my
mother was younger, my grandmother could not afford—literally and figuratively—to have the "problems" of her children get
in her way. She was a very poor woman who worked as a maid

for a White family. On holidays she went to their house and made their dinner before she made my mother's. When one of the Goldberg children was sick she had to tend to them before she could tend to my mother and her siblings. The biggest life lesson that my grandmother wanted to pass on to her children was, when you are Black, you must be able to fight your own battles and figure out what course of action you are going to take, beginning with a certain amount of introspection.

Once my grandmother was cooking, and had blocked the doorway to the kitchen so that her toddlers would not wander into the kitchen and hurt or burn themselves. Well, my mother being the precocious kid that she was, saw a jungle gym instead of a safety device, and she decided that she would jump back and forth over the stool. She succeeded in having fun with this until one time she landed the wrong way and broke her arm. My grandmother gave her a sling and some ice, but she would not take my mother to the hospital. She made my mother sit there on the floor until my reputedly more compassionate grandfather got home from work and took her. This may seem like child abuse. But more than anything else, my mother says that from that moment on, she knew that in all things she would have to figure out how she was going to cope with her own problems. My mother had to learn that my grandmother could not spend her days tending to the bad choices that my mother and her siblings made on occasion. There was simply no time and no money for such things.

Young, black girls growing up in a much less overtly oppressive society, my sister and I still learned this lesson in a variety of ways. Once I had planned a slumber party for my birthday. The invitations had been sent out, and friends were coming over after I got home from school. Unfortunately for me, my nerves and excitement got the best of me, and I developed a stomachache. Instead of taking a little time out of recess to relax and allow myself the chance to really think out all of my options, I insisted on going to the office and having my mother come and pick me up. BIG MISTAKE! My mother told me that if I was too sick to stay at school, then I was too sick to have a slumber party. I, of course, was devastated, and knew that I would be humiliated by having to disinvite my friends from my slumber party. What I had failed to realize was that it cost my mother a tremendous amount of time and work to take off and come get me. I had not factored all of these things into the equation. Just like my mother was forced to sit there in pain because she did not calculate the consequences of jumping over the stool—and the cost to the entire family if my grandmother was interrupted or if she hurt herself—I had not realized that my choice would cost my mother and my family as well.

The net result is that I am a better decision-maker. One of the negative ramifications, however, is that now whenever I have a problem, I sometimes find it hard to reach out for help. There is not only familial pressure to figure things out on your own, but I really feel as though society looks down on black people when they reach out for help. The stereotype of welfare recipients is that they are black women, who don't want to work, who just want to have sex and babies that they cannot afford, when for many women, welfare is only temporary and during difficult times. African and Caribbean women are often viewed as women who are looking for handouts or who are trying to take jobs away from American citizens; not as tax-paying individuals who provide much valuable and needed labor for our country. The Black children in the adoption agencies are considered wards of the state that are more a drain on resources than innocent victims in need of assistance.

I am sure that my grandmother knew that Black people—especially in the south in the early part of the 20th century—should not even begin to consider looking for help from a government which legalized slavery and conferred second class citizenship on Blacks throughout this nation, simply because of the color of their skin. My mother believed that she was the only one who would be there to support her as she struggled to make her way out of poverty. Now I often feel that only I will be able to help take my family and my people into higher echelons of achievement in this country.

Amongst my peers, many of whom have told me that they feel the same way, we often say that we feel as though we carry the weight of the race on our shoulders. This is a heavy and often overwhelming feeling. Sometimes I am paralyzed with a sense that my efforts are useless. Black people face too many systemic obstacles to ever reach true social and economic parity. Other times I am reminded that my grandmother successfully raised seven children who are all in good health, living stable lives, and raising generations more successful than the previous. My mother has achieved phenomenal success for a woman with her childhood disadvantages. And I now attend a top-five law school.

Beyond my personal feelings of powerlessness, there are other issues with the isolationist view of problem solving that many Americans—not just my family—believe in. First of all, I believe that this country does owe a tremendous debt to African-American people. The more this country makes us feel guilty about asking for handouts, the greater our need is masked. In addition, when people are prevented from receiving benefits which they are owed, it causes problems in health care, education, political representation and so many other spheres of life which are integral to success in this nation. Finally, excessive self-reliance creates divides within the African-American community, because often times people who have made it, buy into this whole notion that America does not owe anything to Blacks. That is simply wrong.

In my household, I will say that I get much more support from my mom than she got from hers; and I am sure that I will be even more helpful and communicative with my children. I think (or at least hope) that as time and generations go by, Black people will be able to successfully combine self-reliance and America's payment of reparations. On the one hand, America does owe the Black community a huge debt. At the same time, only with a tremendous amount of reflection, introspection, self-motivation and planning will we be able to demand such reparations and use them in positive ways to reconstruct the Black community and repair the damage that remains from colonialism and slavery.

I grew up in a primarily Latino neighborhood. But it just so happened that my neighbors, who had young daughters, were White. I remember playing with them a lot—typical kid stuff like Barbie, house, etc. I do not ever remember feeling that there were issues with white and black kids playing together. However, once I got older and was more socially involved, I definitely gravitated towards having more Black friends. I spent a tremendous amount of time at my babysitter's house, and she lived in a predominantly Black neighborhood. I think that I have more memories from "Edith's house" than I do of my own house. There, I played with the other mostly Black kids that she babysat and the neighborhood kids. The form of our play changed, mostly because, though she did not live in a poor neighborhood, there simply was not an abundance of toys to play with, like Barbie etc. We used to play lots of tag and make up games where a lot of people could participate.

I spent fourth through sixth grades at a very small private school where I graduated with a class of nine people. For a Beverly Hills school, it is surprising that most of the children in my class were Black. My closest friends were two Black girls and one White girl. I don't think that we treated her any differently, but there were definitely boundaries. For example, I did not spend as much time sleeping over at her place, and I do not think that she ever came to mine. I went to my Black friends' homes often and spent a lot of time with their families. Actually, I think that my White friend, in three years, may have spent one night with me over at Edith's house, and it was a huge deal. I know that she came, but I have no recollection of the things that we did at all. Strange, because I have vivid memories of staying at my Black friends' homes, what we ate and on some occasions what I wore.

I spent seventh through twelfth grades at a private, very wealthy, predominantly White and Asian school (Marlborough school for girls). My seventh grade year my best friend was an Asian girl who was adopted by a white family. I have a lot of fun memories with her, and we were inseparable for a long time. When she moved, our friendship ended. My 8th grade year I was a best friend with a White girl. She was Polish, and I idolized her because she was very smart, an excellent tennis player and very thin. I am not sure why our friendship dwindled. Needless to say, we never spent time together outside of the classroom. I don't think I even knew where she lived.

After these two friendships, I did have some good friends who were White, but I never spent any time with them outside of school. I only hung with Black girls—and eventually I only hung with my Black boyfriend. I am not sure when, but I came to a point where I no longer enjoyed spending my social time with people of other races. It is just easier for me to be Black with other Black people. The White girls at Marlborough were very nice to me and definitely respected me—I was (eventually) thin, had long hair and a pretty face, I danced on our school's dance team, and had just enough attitude to entertain, but not threaten, them. I eventually went on to be the school's third Black student body president in over 100 years of history. I don't even think they let us in before about 1975. I kept social and emotional distance between myself and the other non-Black girls because I simply did not trust them very much. I had no reason to. I recently spoke to a Jewish girl who graduated from Marlborough with my sister. She is very "liberal" and into social justice. She told me that when she was at Marlborough she was always at the center of controversy, and causing problems at the school because she hated the fact that it was such a blatantly elitist, White institution. I am still not sure why she did not demand that her parents take her out of the school, but I suppose that is another conversation. Anyway, she asked me, "Didn't you just hate how White and oppressive the whole environment was." I had to tell her, "no." I do not expect for White people to be anything other than oppressive and White. I had no other expectations for them, so they did not surprise me. I just played the game, let them love me for the superficial reasons that they did. At the sound of the bell, I left and let Marlborough and its issues stay at 250 South Rossmore.

My mom became very active at the school once I became student body president. At one meeting, another mother asked her, "So how do you think Kerri went on to become student body president?" The presumption was that I could not have done it like any of the other hundred or so White girls that had done it. I was the exception, and not the rule. And she simply could not understand what made me so exceptional. I think the only thing that explains my success was my ability to play the game in a way that I did not allow White people to surprise me—I always expected the worst, and I did just fine. Set the bar just a little bit higher for me, and I will make out okay.

I must say that I thoroughly enjoyed my time at that school. I would definitely send my daughter there. It provided me with a very valuable education and friends (Black ones) that I will have forever. But by my last quarter there, I thought that the White girls were going to drive me crazy. Looking back, I realized that 6 years of turning the other cheek was starting to wear on me; and I simply needed to be out of there. Nonetheless, if I had it to do all over again, I would do the same thing and make the same choices.

My decision to go to UC Berkeley was simple—it had an excellent reputation, it was inexpensive, it was close to home and my sister had loved her years there. I knew it was predominantly White. But, I also knew that a niche in the Black community—no matter how small—was waiting for me.

I must say that I loved my years at Berkeley. The White people stayed the same. I insulated myself in the Black community. Despite their larger numbers, I do not think that I really had one good White friend. I have no problem working with, talking to, or interacting with White people; and I do enjoy their thoughts and insights on some academic issues. I once wrote on an exam, on which I got an F, that the only thing that White people can offer me is scientific knowledge (I included law and other sorts of professional fields within my definition of science). To a certain extent I still think that this is true. I think that I could go on living my life perfectly content to interact personally and socially with Black people. I know that there must be something that I am missing out on, but I have yet to find out or even glimpse what it may be.

David
Spring 1998

I was born and raised in Brentwood, Long Island New York, a working class community comprised mostly of Italians, Jews, Puerto Ricans and Blacks. As a small child, race and class were not major issues to me. I do remember some kids walking around the street bare foot, but I just thought they were dirty. It never crossed my mind that their parents couldn't afford shoes. Some kids in the neighborhood would always come to my house asking for food, and my mother loved feeding them. We never asked questions as to why they didn't eat at home; that was just what we did. If someone was at the house playing with me and they were hungry, my mother would prepare them a plate.

My mother also came from a poor background, born and raised in Jamaica. She was the youngest of three girls. She was sent to the United States at age seventeen to work and earn money for her family. Upon arrival in New York City she met my father and decided to stay.

My father's parents were Venezuelan and Trinidadian; his mother was of African decent, and his father was of Spanish/Carib Indian decent. They migrated to the United States in the 1920's from

Trinidad. My father is one of four children; he was born in New York City in 1930. His family was poor, but worked very hard.

I had one friend who lived next door; he was a White boy named Joseph. As kids we were the best of friends, but once we hit junior high, race became a major issue. He stopped "hanging out" with me and only played with other White kids in the neighborhood. His new friends did not care for me and would yell out racial slurs anytime that I rode my bike past their house. It was not long before we became enemies; I hung out with the Blacks and Puerto Ricans, while Joseph stuck with the White kids. We would fight over use of the baseball field at the neighborhood park and bike trails in the area. One time they caught me riding my bike alone and jumped me. One mother watched everything happen through her window and did nothing. When I went home with cuts and bruises, my older brother was not pleased. He told me to ride down the street again and he would hide in the bushes to see if they tried to do anything again. Sure enough they did, as they threw me off my bike, my brother came running down the block and began throwing them off me. He didn't hurt anyone, but made it clear that they should leave me alone. At that point the same mother that watched me get jumped came outside telling him to leave her kids alone. She didn't care that I was the one with the cuts and bruises, only that my brother was scaring her kids. Within minutes after that event, the police, parents and a whole bunch of White kids came knocking at my door. They threatened to arrest my brother if he touched those kids again. To make a long story short, I hated that place.

My move to California at age fourteen was very refreshing. It took me a while to open up to White kids, due to past experiences. I was shocked to see Black and White kids hanging out together at Berkeley High. Life in California was nothing like New York; racism was not as blatant, it came across subtler and that was fine with me.

As a whole my family does not communicate very often due to the vast distances between where we live. Some are in

New York, others are in Florida, the Caribbean, and a few remain in California. However, when new news breaks, it spreads like a virus. For example, a few months ago I called an aunt in NYC to inquire as to where in the city I could go to shop for engagement rings. She then called my father in Miami to tell him that I was buying a ring. He took it upon himself to call my brothers in California to tell them that I had purchased a ring and three days later I got a call from my sister in Trinidad saying "Mommy is upset with you for not personally telling her that you were engaged." Now mind you, I still had not bought the ring. This just goes to show that my family thrives on gossip, but never gets the information accurate.

I personally did not experience any problems with African Americans, but that is largely due to that fact that I was born in the USA; many of my experiences growing up are similar to those of African Americans. However, if you spoke to my parents you would get a different response. They were born and raised in the Caribbean and grew up learning many negative stereotypes of African Americans (i.e., lazy, not trustworthy, etc.).

On the other hand I have met many middle class African Americans who look down on West Indians. Their belief is that they (West Indians) have no class, drink a lot of alcohol, and run around bare foot. Ironic as it may sound, I'm marrying a middle class Black woman and I can't wait until our families meet one another at the wedding.

One thing I have felt is discrimination from some Mexican Americans. They look down on me because I have a Spanish name, but look Black. In New York its no big deal because both Puerto Ricans and Dominicans look like me, but in California, that was not the case. The Mexicans would intentionally pronounce my name in English rather than Spanish.

When it came to choosing a college, I wanted to attend a school with a top name that was not very expensive and would enable me to be near my mother. UC Berkeley ranked at the top of my list and with three of my siblings having previously attended the school, it was an easy decision to make. Overall, I would say that I loved my experience at Cal. There was never an awkward moment. In the beginning, I had my high school friends to rely on when I didn't know anyone. By the second year, I was in a fraternity and made four very close friends through that process. In addition, I was involved in a number of on-campus and off-campus activities, which enabled me to make friends with a variety of people. Through rugby, I made friends with White people; at West Indian parties, I made friends with Africans and West Indians; and from living in Berkeley and Oakland, I had friends who were homeless, poor, street performers and activists. Berkeley is a very open and accepting community to people of all kinds. My experience at Cal and living in Berkeley helped define my views on life. It was almost too good to be true, because now that I live in upstate New York in a small town that is mostly White, I really miss the diversity of Berkeley.

I'm a very curious person and I knew that many "touchy" issues would arise in class, issues that you don't normally have the chance to discuss with people. This is why I wanted to be a part of the class, to learn more about other cultures and get others' perspective and views on life. The first day of class I thought to myself "here we have the rainbow coalition." It was great: we had Indians, Whites, Blacks, Latinos and Asians. It is not often that you can get that many different types of people together in one classroom, even at a large university like Cal.

One lesson I learned from this class was that despite people's many differences, if given the chance, we really could all get along. It's just that sometimes people get locked in their ways and comfortable with their social groups, so they choose not to interact with new and different people. This class is a great way to make friends and meet people of all types. It would be an ideal freshman seminar to break students into Berkeley's diversity before they get locked in their ways. For many upperclassmen, it is already too late.

Tel

Fall 1999

In 1896 Homer Plessy brought suit against the state of Louisiana in Plessy v. Ferguson. Plessy contended that the Jim Crow statute, which required racially segregated seating on interstate trains, was unconstitutional. The Supreme Court quickly ruled against the plaintiff, and this case became the basis for the "separate but equal" doctrine that was central to justifying all Jim Crow legislation created during the next 58 years. Essentially, Plessy v. Ferguson codified what was already common knowledge: there is a traditional boundary between the two socio-cultural groups designated white and nonwhite. Today, although legal justification is nonexistent, similar Jim Crowesque segregation exists in every facet of life from neighborhoods to schools.

As a student at U.C. Berkeley, the so-called "most diverse" student population in the world, I have observed more racialized spatial segregation than a cotton plantation in mid-July! While people of color are not explicitly discouraged from joining fraternities and sororities, the unbelievably low number of people that actually do participate would suggest otherwise. Similarly, it is immediately apparent which sports are for people of color and which are not. The number of Blacks on the rugby team during the past three years has remained a consistent one; I should know because I am that individual. Consistently, over the past semester I was the only Black male in two of my four classes. And the classes where I wasn't alone were both African American Studies courses (hardly surprising). How can we begin to talk about an equal playing field when even the flagship for diversity in education, U.C. Berkeley, has joined the ranks of the pernicious oppressors?

People of color have been told that there's a crisis in our community, there's an emergency situation...crime is rampant and out of control. California voters believe (and it is apparent that they truly believe this because of their overwhelming approval of

Proposition 21) that the only way to eliminate this crisis is to build 22,000 new prison spaces over the next 30 years at the cost of nearly a billion dollars. There is a crisis then, there's definitely a crisis and a big one—you might call it the biggest crisis in the history of the state of California. But the real emergency is not crime, it's not even gang membership, the real emergency is prejudiced legislation that guarantees people of color are treated as inferior. The real emergency is naive people who don't believe legislation is a life or death matter. Institutional racism has killed more people of color than every act of the Ku Klux Klan combined. IF YOU'RE NOT FIGHTING RACISM YOU ARE RACISM!

While generalizations are usually more detrimental than effective, and often catalyze cyclical stupidity, it is sometimes necessary to use them. In the Ethnic Studies class I was able to more clearly understand the "White position" on racial stratification, and why it is unbelievably egocentric and naive. White justification of contemporary oppression seems to fall into two categories. First, Whites argue: "What could I possibly do to show you that I understand the struggles of people of color and I want to help?" Whites argue that no matter what they do, they cannot be accepted. This is not true. Acceptance will come, but only when Whites stop believing that menial efforts like tutoring a student after school will stop the tidal wave of oppression. It is easy to try and make a difference when you go home to a huge house at night. If we understand that every single day hundreds die because of the "concentration effects" that are catalyzed in ghetto communities, we realize that minor changes will never stop the unbelievably huge prejudice of our society. Even Malcolm X, who is often labeled a reverse racist, argued that there was one White man who made a difference. Malcolm X argued that John Brown's murder of dozens of slave owners at a revolt on Harper's Ferry highlighted his true commitment to equality for all people. John Brown was actively doing all he could (to the point that he lost his life) to change the society he saw, because racism was, and still is, a life or death matter. Many Whites, and people of color too, have money. Wealth is not inherently bad, but because of globalization every single person who is rich does so at the expense of someone else. And in the New World economy, every single American above the poverty line is rich. We must all realize that people paid well under minimum wage provide all our clothes, cars, electronics, and food. That is not justice.

The next argument generally put forth by Whites is, "But some people of color are not doing all they could be doing either, so it's not just a White/Black thing, it's a bad/good thing." It is hard for me to hold someone who is impoverished to the same standards that I hold someone who is educated, recognizes what is going on, and still refuses to do anything. Similarly, there is going to be a time soon that people of color, both in the US and abroad, will become so impoverished that they demand rights (probably violently). It is at this time that those Whites and people of color, who both do equally little to change society, will part ways. For example, a White person may believe in affirmative action. But if a revolution were to begin and that person realized that her family, her sorority sisters, her friends, her acquaintances, and everything she had ever known was a facet of the western, capitalist, bourgeoisie, elitist system, she would find it tough to go against that system. I know that this is something I struggle with everyday. I am at one of the most elite universities in the world, and I recognize that almost everything I believe has its basis in Western ideology. What is different about Whites and people of color, for the most part, is I have been treated terribly by the system and so have many of my family and friends. The White friends I have are either down for the cause or they are not truly my friends. When it comes down to a life or death situation for change, I won't have to worry about taking sides against my friends because they will be there with me.

Algernol
Fall 1987

I was raised in a single mother home. My mother was born in 1929 in Louisiana. She was a product of southern racism, but she tried very desperately to make my life different. I grew up in South Central Los Angeles—at the time, a predominantly Black community. My school didn't teach me anything about being Black except that my people were slaves who ran away on the Underground Railroad. By the time I made it to 6th grade, I knew that the school I was attending and my teacher were prejudiced. I had no problem handling the kids outside, but I couldn't handle the injustice from my teachers.

My mother also helped me in some of my self-awareness by giving me books to read like Roots, Nat Turner, Harriet Tubman, Uncle Tom's Cabin, Black Boy, and Malcolm X.

I wanted to go to a campus where I could be a student first, and then an athlete. I didn't want to go somewhere like Wyoming where I would mainly play football. When I arrived on the campus, I had a big chip on my shoulder. I wanted others to know that I got to this campus purely on academics, and yes, I was also a good football player. I found out more and more that I had to wear my SAT scores and GPA on my chest. "Yes my GPA was 3.7 at a private school, and I scored 1200 on my SAT." I found myself having to defend Affirmative Action everywhere I went.

The Ethnic Studies class was the best class that I had ever taken. I learned so much about diversity, and I learned that this world wasn't just Black and White. I always wanted to be in a utopia type setting around race, where we could all come together and really get along, and live in America sharing the same nationality as Americans. This class made it possible for me to believe that such a utopia could happen, but only through a lot of work.

As I ventured out into the world, I have proudly stepped into the battle to make things better around me, and have been very involved in doing community work from planting trees to teaching kids in some of the toughest neighborhoods. Presently I'm a special education teacher teaching pupils who were labeled severely emotional disturbed.

My commitment to the Black community stems from a sense of empowering our youth with the knowledge of how to be successful in the U.S., and to make this country be true to the ideals that were set forth. I have been fortunate enough to spend my professional career working in the Black community through various organizations by sharing my education with my "gente." I basically see myself as a strong African American male, who has been blessed with getting a great education, and is part of "Dubois's Talented Tenth," helping to make my community part of the American community, and closing the gaps of intolerance so we all can truly be Americans. So I'm very committed to the Black community, but no less committed to being an American, which means whatever I do, I want it to work for everybody. I want to empower as well as embrace all of America. This idea is what makes me a strong American, and the rest of my society needs to learn this to share in my American dream of making this country great for all.

One thing that I know is that this society is as racist as it is sexist, and so many groups are put on the chopping block to hate. We need more classes like this to start teaching others that diversity is a good thing. One does not need to hate to validate oneself. Love starts within, and then love can be shared. I'm an African American, and I love myself, so I have no problem loving you no matter what religion, race, creed, gender, or sexual orientation you may be. I don't blame any particular group for my condition because I have the power to make changes. If you want to sit on the side and be a whiner, then you will always lose in life. When you decide to help make things better, then you already won. This class helped me become a winner, and I will utilize the knowledge and wisdom that I gained in my endeavors for my community.

Taryn Clark
Spring 1996

I went with a classmate to Chinatown in Oakland for lunch. Mid-way through lunch, my classmate got a disturbed look on her face but she wouldn't tell me why. I later found out that one of the waiters had called me a Black devil in another language. I was of course offended and wished she had told me earlier, but I guess she didn't want to cause a scene. But that was a clear indication of the prejudice and hate that people have towards me just because of the way I look. I also want this incident to serve as an example of why people get upset sometimes when other people talk in another language around them. Many people often think that those who do not understand the language are just oversensitive and paranoid, but this served as proof that we have a right to be paranoid because people will talk about you right under your nose.

European Americans

"One of the worst parts of the class for me was being told that I was "the white man," that I was just as responsible for the racism and horrible actions that people in my race had committed against people of color as the people who committed them were…the students argued…everyone had to take responsibility or nothing could be changed…I was yelled at, I cried and was defiant, and finally, after months, I understood."

—Daisy, Spring 1997

I'm Not Black, or What Do You Say When You're White?

I am not you.
You are not me.
We differ and differ we do well.
I can sympathize until i'm blue, but
black i'll never be—
because i am not you and
you are not me.
I didn't bring you over on a ship
but white society's long preserved whip
still leaves scars and often, too, open wounds on your back.
I hope some day not to see
me against you or
you against me,

but a mutual respect between us—not as us and them,
but as we.
I cannot un-do that which is done, but still I
ask for your forgiveness—
not for the color of my skin, but for the
colors of my past.
We both must move on
me accepting you accepting me,
accepting ourselves and each other in unison,
both forgiving the human slaughter and mental slander
of my not too distant past.
But while we both forgive out of love,
we must never forget.
For if hindsight is truly 20/20,
let us both look back just once
and forever march onward hand in hand,
black and white,
me and you—different both—toward change.

—*Kelly, Spring 1988*

Daisy
Spring 1997

I grew up, the youngest of three girls in Brentwood, an affluent neighborhood of Los Angeles. My sisters and I are all blonde haired and blue eyed—Scandinavian looking. My parents were from Chicago and had moved out to Los Angeles, taking many of their values and opinions with them. Both were fairly open-minded, and I certainly never heard pejorative talk about people of other races in open conversation. However, my father had been an elected Republican politician in Chicago, and he and my mother shared what could be considered "conservative" view-points on a range of issues.

I think that there were two main themes that created my personal views on race. The first was the conservative background and highly charged political discussions that dominated the dinner table; the second was the socio-economic environment in which I grew up. The two seemed to go hand in hand. Because my father had the record of being an elected official, for many years I felt his views must be correct. I don't mean to say that I was indoctrinated in his views, but rather that I felt they held credence because of his record. Early on, my parents taught us how fortunate we girls were to grow up in such a comfortably affluent household, and both had come from comfortable families themselves.

I never felt like I was one of "those," the privileged class that was so prevalent in my community. I think this was important in forming my views and making me see life more realistically than many of my friends although I still had quite a skewed perception of normalcy. For example, our housekeeper only came 2 times a week, whereas most of my friends had live-ins. I thought that was a little ridiculous although we had live-ins to help my mom while the three of us (my sisters and I) were younger. I remember getting older in high school and many of my friends passing on old clothes to their housekeeper or housekeeper's children. It seemed like charity and though unspoken, there was a feeling that the housekeeper was lucky to receive such gifts. Perhaps it wouldn't be so odd to think except for the fact that almost all of the housekeepers were Latina. There was an underlying feeling that they were lucky to get good jobs with such generous families. Such subtle views were the kind that many of our family friends held. However, I really had no day-to-day exposure to people of different races except for the few people of color who were in my high school and who seemed to have everything I had. That was the second unspoken—that as long as the people of color had the money and education, and didn't celebrate their race, that they were not considered minorities. There was little value given to race because no one, especially not the people of color in my high school, called attention to it.

Throughout high school, I took Japanese for 4 years to fulfill the language requirement. My first experience with first-hand racism came not from my seeing a non-White friend in Los Angeles being a victim of it, but from my being aware of it on a summer trip to Japan. I stayed for 6 weeks with my oldest sister in a small town and can honestly say it was the first time I'd ever felt different in a way that indicated that certain things were not open to me because of my race and gender. Any tourist in any foreign country can tell stories of walking into a locals-only place and being told it's closed. Likewise, I would be stared at, discouraged to go places, told that I couldn't get a job when I was older except for maybe teaching or something more traditionally womanly.

Many of the boundaries I bumped up against were not real barriers to anything I really wanted to do; rather I was given evasive answers and suggestions about options I might want to consider choosing in the future. It was extremely subtle, but I felt unwanted. When I sat down to write my UC application, I found that my experiences with racism and sexism in the Japanese homogenous society were some of the most thought provoking experiences I'd had, and I wrote my essay on those. I think that I had started to identify, in some small way with what other people must feel, even though I had no real contact with people of different races other than my family's housekeeper.

My oldest sister had gone to Berkeley and loved it, so it was natural that I go as well. It was the first public school I'd ever gone to in my life. My freshman year, I lived in the dorms with a Chinese American girl who I will never forget. She had grown up first generation in Chinatown in San Francisco and was incredibly sheltered, quiet and sweet. I noticed how she would go home every weekend because it seemed it was expected of her, how diligently she studied, and how high her goals were (she's presently in medical school). Her parents barely spoke English and had hardly assimilated into America despite the fact that her family lived in California since she was born. She had never been outside of San Francisco, never had a boyfriend, never had a drink, nor ever spoke of doing anything reckless. I was certainly not a boisterous person, but I was on the phone with friends, I joined a sorority, and I would regularly go eat in the dining hall with male friends. Such actions emphasized the difference in our upbringings and made each of us open our eyes. I remember being extremely embarrassed to come home late or if I'd been to a party where alcohol had been provided. She did not judge me, but I could see how I was just as much of a culture shock to her as she was to me. It was a good experience. I became very sensitive; trying not to make her uncomfortable with everything I'd grown up with and taken for granted—both materially and in terms of values and expectations.

The rest of my time at Berkeley, I lived in a nearly all White sorority that was home to many affluent girls. We did not pay much more than your average Cal student pays for housing, but we had generous accounts at our disposal to cover the more major expenses through the sorority's boards. We had cooks and a maintenance staff, and an absolutely beautiful house. I threw myself into extra-curricular activities such as student government and city boards where I gained a perspective on what people thought of the Greek system and what the actual facts were. Its reputation, from what I gathered, was that it was predominantly White, it had double standards for men and women, its students were more affluent than average students, and its members used their connections after college to get good jobs and keep the whole networking/friendship circle going. It was falsely perceived to be a way to keep everybody else who wasn't White and rich out of the whole game, even after graduation. Aside from these rumors, I really enjoyed it and became president of my sorority my senior year. Though it had been easy to ignore the rumors before, as president, I was responsible for public relations and any problems that might occur to damage the reputation of the Greek system and my particular house.

One of the most difficult problems to deal with was the Latino cultural house that abutted our courtyard. When the girls in my house were loud, the neighbors would yell "slurs." When they would play their music loudly, the girls in my house would yell or make disparaging comments about their culture. There had never been a good relationship between the two houses, both because no one knew anyone in either house personally, and because the perceptions were so imbedded. Most of the girls in my house didn't even understand that it was a Latino cultural house. Compared to our house, it was always less maintained and noisy, and many of our residents were judgmental about it. They would ask why they didn't clean it up or why they had to listen to their music and yell all of the time. In reality, it was subsidized housing and the funds just weren't there to connect parts of the house, so people would yell from one end to another. But instead of finding the answers, many of the girls, myself included, would just jump to conclusions that they were messy and loud.

My senior year, I was introduced to the interracial relations class at Cal. I've always thought of myself as an open-minded person, and I've always had a hard time saying "no" when asked to participate in something. However, I did not like some of what I considered to be the almost militant slant of the ethnic studies department at UC Berkeley. Granted Proposition 187 was still on the minds of many students. When I was approached about the class, I didn't like the personal questions; I didn't like the assumption that probing would uncover racist feelings. But when I was challenged, when the question was asked "am I making you uncomfortable with these questions," I realized that I probably could benefit from the interracial relations class. I figured that the reason I was uncomfortable was because I thought I had something to hide, and I have never felt comfortable with that feeling. So I took the leap, expecting to listen and lightly talk my way through the class, letting the other students see how open-minded I thought I was. It wasn't that easy.

The first few weeks of the class were absolutely fascinating to me. I felt like I was watching a daytime talk show. The students would speak about their lives in all honesty. It was not confrontational, and everyone seemed interested in everyone else's stories. However, as we made our way around the group in the next few weeks, people started tiring of listening to other people's stories and started challenging them with tough questions and insinuating remarks. It began to get confrontational. The first week, we had an assignment to visit the home of a person in the class who was of a different race and gender. I went over to M—'s house. He was Latino and a political science major, like me. We were to read or share something important to us. He read me a series of statistics on consumption and how the average American is willing to spend more money per year on his/her pet than it would take to feed a homeless person for a year. The statistics were all very identifiable and plagued my conscious. I don't remember what I showed him or read to him. M— and I talked for a while that day, and he became a friend in the class. Highly intelligent, he'd been the son of migrant farm workers and had grown up helping his parents in the summers. He wanted to study diligently while at Cal and then make an impact and help his community once he established himself. This was quite different from other people in the class who considered themselves activists already. His idea was less threatening to me and more in line with my beliefs. Although I later came to understand the importance of activism, I still appreciate and believe that M—'s way can be equally effective to influence change in a community. I guess you have to have both types of people in this world, but I believe that M—'s way of helping his community will make him a leader across communities.

One of the worst parts of the class for me was being told that I was "the white man," that I was just as responsible for the racism and horrible actions that people in my race had committed against people of color as the people who committed them. I didn't take well to this. My idea was that those people had been bad people, let the blame fall on them. They were the enemy. Many of the students didn't agree. They argued that that was ridiculous and believed that everyone had to take responsibility for his or her race because that was the only way that oppression could effectively be fought. This, I finally came to understand. I was yelled at; I cried and was defiant. Finally, after months, I understood. I think the lesson was that everyone is responsible for taking blame, for accepting racism or for fighting against it. You cannot turn a blind eye and be innocent. You cannot find a racist joke funny or consider yourself not racist because "you have a Black friend." And I also learned that *everyone* is racist—even the most adamant civil rights leaders. Everyone is a work-in-progress, trying to undo the assumptions, fears, and experience we grew up with in our culture.

As one of the homework assignments, I went over to the Latino house next door to my sorority to prepare dinner, serve the residents, and clean up afterward. I met a lot of people and really had a good time with them. They seemed very surprised that I was doing what I was doing being that I lived in the sorority next door. Only one of the girls treated me badly, ordering me around the kitchen. I knew that the reason I was taking this assignment was to have a glimpse into what it felt like to be a busboy at a restaurant or to do a job that paid a pittance while having an education that merited more. I think that since I understood this was a one-night educational experience and since they knew I was a student at Berkeley, it wasn't as effective as it could have been.

That night, just as dinner ended, Jenny, a girl in the class, asked if I wanted to go back to her room to observe a ceremony involving drums. I had heard the drums from my sorority and had thought it was strange. When I went into her room with a couple of other residents, she explained to me the cultural and historical significance behind the drumming. We lit incense and she performed the ceremony. I realized how awful it would have been at that moment if someone from the sorority had interrupted with a remark yelled across the courtyard. Having no idea that the students next door were performing a ceremony, we just thought they were being loud. The ceremony was fascinating, and it definitely opened my eyes. When we came out of the room, I was told that some people in the house were mad at me. According to what I was told, they thought I had shirked my duties because I thought I was better than they were or because I was spoiled. I hadn't meant to not help clean up but when Jenny asked me to come to her room, I thought it would be rude to say no to her. I had learned a lot in her room. She tried to explain to the others but I do not think it was very effective. I felt like I could do no right by them. And that is the whole point. After years of perceptions, you cannot change people's minds about you in one night, just as you cannot change your mind about other races and cultures in one night or in one semester.

By the end of the class, I think I had grown a lot. I had made friends with people in the class with whom I really didn't have much in common with, but I understood their lives and feelings. It was a superficial friendship in some ways, but also very deep. The most important lesson I learned from the class was that sure, it was great that I finally "got it," but that didn't matter— what mattered was what I did with it going forward. Judging by the statistics pertaining to my education, and family background, I'd learned that I had a better shot at rising through the traditional ranks of business and to be in a position to make a difference than many other people in the class. As much as I worry about my future, I know that I have family and financial support, parents with higher degrees to push me and serve as role models, and White skin. The hope is, that when I do get in a position where I am setting the rules for a company or group of people, I'll take what I've learned from the class and move forward to make a difference. At the very least, I think that I owe it to myself and to the people who opened up to me in the class. I don't think it's fair that I might have a better shot of making it in life just because of what I was born into. As a way of evening things out, the least I can do going forward is try to help out those who have been hindered by racial or cultural barriers.

John
Fall 1993

My father's parents were of Norwegian descent, the Olson and Andersen families. Their parents came to the United States in the late 1800's and lived among the growing Scandinavian population in Minnesota. My grandfather was a Lutheran minister, and my grandmother was an English teacher. They moved to Iowa where my father was born in 1930. They were, I suppose, upper middle class.

My experience at Cal was mostly a positive one. I learned a lot about myself and experienced my share of growing pains as I matured and I became more aware of my place in the world and myself. In particular, I became much more aware of the experience of ethnic minorities and the poor in Berkeley, the US, and the world. This, at times, was an uncomfortable experience, as my perceptions of social issues and most importantly my perception of myself changed radically.

One of the ways this manifested itself was my experience in the Greek system. I was the president of my fraternity and then president of the Interfraternity Council, so to many I was the symbol of the Greek system—I was identified inextricably with it. To many, the Greek system was, and is, an institution of privilege for rich White people. Certainly the history of the Greek system might lead one to believe this, and while the system was more diverse and tolerant than it had been, I saw many examples of how this was still true. For many fraternity men, the Greek system was an elite bastion where one was protected from dealing with issues of race and class. I wrestled with my own role in this system, and while I did what I could to address these concerns (perhaps not everything I could), I was left with many questions and concerns about what role the Greek system was playing in the lives of students.

One of my pet theories about the Greek system (which occurred to me during the class) is that fraternities are clans or groups for young men who don't have an identifiable clan or group to belong to. Most Whites in America have had their ancestral cultural practices squeezed out of them by the American notion of the melting pot, in which everyone is the same. I think very few White people practice native cultural traditions, like language or rituals, of their ancestors. My Norwegian and Irish heritages are barely recognizable anywhere but through my name. I think also that there is something in the nature of being human that draws us to people who are like us, and calls us to live as a part of an identifiable group that is separate from other groups. For people of color, these groups are readily identifiable. For Whites, the groups need to be artificially constructed because the clans of our ancestors have been washed away by Ellis Island. Fraternities and sororities, then, are artificial clans that allow the members to claim identity in a group, with its own rituals, ideals, even clothing.

Indeed, it was my role as a leader in the Greek system that led to my being recommended for the class. By the time I took the class, my views had changed considerably so I was very open to the opportunity of being in the class, and looked forward to the experience.

What surprised me most about the class, and I think the most important thing I learned from it, was that my understanding of what it is like to be a person of color is necessarily limited. I thought of myself as someone who understood of the issues that face communities of color, and I thought I was on the "right" side of the issue. I discovered though, as the class progressed that as a White man I could never *truly* understand how the world feels from the perspective of a person of color. I can be sympathetic,

I can listen, I can learn, I can even try to contribute to the cause, but my point of view is mine, and is formed not only by who I am as a person but by how the world treats me as a person. This treatment is different than the treatment that people from other backgrounds receive.

This realization was uncomfortable at first, because I wanted to think of myself as a person who *can* identify with the experience of communities of color. I realized that what people of color were expecting from their White brothers was not a complete understanding of their experience, for they knew this was impossible, but rather an open mind. They expected attentive listening to their stories, even if the stories made me uncomfortable. It wasn't my responsibility to understand the experience; it was my responsibility to listen, above all else, and then to do my best to understand and even take action by being involved in my community.

Warren
Spring 1991

I am not aware of being of any particular "class." However, statistics would indicate that my family is wealthy. Over time, my dad had success in the real estate business, but it didn't cross my mind that we were any particular class. Likewise, I was never aware of my race until I came to Cal.

Both sets of my grandparents are white, American, and grew up comfortably. My immediate family is extremely close. All of us not only get along well but like spending time together. My parents are still happily married after 33 years and having raised four children (all of whom went to Cal). All the members of our family live in the Bay Area except me. I am attending business school in Chicago.

We are fairly close to our extended family on my dad's side. Almost all our aunts, uncles, and cousins live within a couple of miles of my parents. Most of them went to Cal. We see each other every Thanksgiving, Christmas, and Easter. Some of my cousins are closer than others—usually dictated by age. We are not as close with the members of my mom's family. The main reason is that they live in Southern California. Before my mom's parents died we visited at least once a year, and they would come to Northern California once a year. Since then we don't see them as often. My mom still remains close with them and visits as often as she can to see her four siblings.

Family dinners are still a frequent event for all holidays, for each family member's birthday, and when we can find the time. We spend a week together every Christmas for some kind of vacation. How often we see each other tends to vary by season (strange, I know). In the fall, my brother and I see my parents frequently on weekends because we hunt ducks together. We are now starting to see my sister more often as her husband has picked up hunting. During the summer, we all often see each other in Lake Tahoe.

I never wanted to go anywhere else but Cal. I was raised going to Cal football games as a kid. Both my parents and almost all my aunts and uncles went to Cal. While there was no pressure to go to Cal, I always assumed I would. I never really thought about any other school. The experience was fantastic. I grew and changed immensely. I got a better understanding of the real, and sometimes harsh, world. I enjoyed myself thoroughly, but became tougher at the same time.

My closest friends were a bunch of my fraternity brothers and a group of women from some sororities. The group of about 14–15 of us became very close over the years, and we continue to be close to this day. Most of these friends are white. I had few friends at Cal who were minorities, not surprising since few of my fraternity brothers were minorities. Several minority groups had their own Greek System and own chapters, which attracted many of the minorities from Cal.

At Cal, I became aware of race and diversity in both good and bad forms. The school is more diverse than where I grew up. There were signs in store windows with Help Wanted—Priority given to Minority Applicants. I was "jumped" on two occasions by roaming groups of thugs yelling racial slurs.

Ultimately, I took the class, which allowed me to hear the unspoken emotions that are prevalent in a school as diverse as Cal. I am aware of my family's financial success but never thought of it as a privilege. My dad has worked hard for everything he has achieved, and his success has been entirely self-made. I never felt that anyone perceived me differently.

I didn't really know anything about the class before taking it. Another student recommended me. The class sounded interesting, and so I took it...it ended up being the best class I took at Cal. I don't recall being struck by the other members of the class as much as I was by the small size of the class and the layout of the room—beanbags, couches, etc. It wasn't until we started covering the various topics of the class that I really got to know my classmates. I have many memorable moments from the class.

Class "homework" was typically an interactive assignment that allowed you to experience some part of a culture. I always volunteered for homework where food was involved. One of the assignments was to have a meal at Soul Brother's Kitchen in Oakland. I was the only white person in the restaurant. I sat at the counter and ordered the fried chicken. The cook/cashier was friendly, but I couldn't help but feel like all the customers were staring at me. I felt out of place. I felt awkward. I'll never forget the feeling.

Students in the class were brutally honest. When the white students were responsible for hosting the class on our culture one of my classmates asked, "What is white culture? You don't have a culture." During our final retreat, one of my white classmates summarized/asked, "Why can't we all just view each other and treat each other equally?" A student from the other section (the class had two sections) whom I didn't know responded, "Maybe we all don't want to be equal. Maybe, we want to be where you are now. And if you ask me, the day is coming where we're going to revolt and you all better look out behind you!" This honesty and emotion typified our typical class.

Sometimes, the lessons I learned in class were simply common sense rather than controversial. A woman once remarked how intimidating and uncomfortable it was to have someone come walking up behind her on the street (especially at night or when the streets were secluded) because she couldn't see who it was and would become frightened. Since then I have always made it a point to walk directly to the right or left of a woman when walking on the sidewalk, always keeping myself as distant and visible as possible.

During one class, a classmate stated, "I don't want any help. I don't want any handouts. Just get out of my way. I can do it on my own." (From that point forward, I was always impressed by this classmate.)

During our final retreat the group consensus was that it was not okay for white people to "label" minorities. In other words, it wasn't fair to generalize about a race. Likewise, it was not deemed OK for minorities to label one another. Nonetheless, the consensus was that it was okay for minorities to "warn" that white people were "like this" or "like that" because it was a way to protect themselves. This was difficult for me to understand and even harder to accept.

This class was an eye-opening experience for me. It was not always positive. It was real. I saw people cry, and I saw real anger. Often, there was frustration. Often there was exasperation. I covered this range of emotions several times over the duration of the course. I am the kind of person that likes solutions. This course left no closure for me. In hindsight, I don't think any was intended. I believe the class set people out to strive to do better in their own actions and possibly to influence others to do the same. I have come away with a more realistic expectation of what "others" may want...I have no clue what other people want! Instead,

I try to not to stereotype or assume that the way I view things is the same as the way someone else may view them.

I walked away with some concrete lessons. I try to evaluate others as individuals not as members of a race, sex, or group. This pertains to both positive and negative stereotypes. The lesson that stuck with me the most is the comment, "Get out of my way, I can do it myself." By continuing to evaluate others as individuals rather than a member of a class, race or group, I do my own thing. Rather than try to "help," I have followed the advice of my classmate…I have simply gotten out of the way.

Native Americans

"The people in power set it up good. They don't want to talk about slavery or government treaties; 'all that is in the past,' they say with a straight face. Instead, they direct your attention to a puddle at your feet, saying, 'Look at that! What are we gonna do about that puddle?' and you're standing there staring into that puddle when there is an ocean behind you."
—Paul, Fall 1999

Anthony
Spring 2000

My parents and grandparents are Native American. We consider ourselves to be Indians. Our class would be labeled "poverty" by the dominant society's structure. My grandparents were not citizens until the 1924 Indian Citizenship Act. Most of my aunt's and uncles were born without birth certificates. I always tell people that I am a second-generation citizen; however, carbon dated materials have proven that my tribe has existed in the region where I am from for over 14,000 years.

We interact with each other as one family unit. This includes extended family. For the most part, we stick up and around for each other. Our grandparents, great aunts, etc. hold the family together. The women especially play an important role in the structure of the family and its longevity.

At an early age, I was very aware of my race and class. In elementary school, I used to get teased a lot for looking different. Most of the teasing came from older White students. They loved

24 Hour Notice
to
Vacate Premises

The University of California, Berkeley is trespassing upon indigenous lands. The United Indigenous Nations do hereby declare that these premises are to be vacated within a 24- hour period. All property, buildings, along with the land, will revert back to the original guardians: the Native people of California. Any wealth accumulated by non-Indigenous people during their stay here will be reclaimed and will remain here (where it belongs). Arrangements have been made, and a ship will dock in the Alameda and San Francisco Bay for the immediate deportation of all non-Indigenous persons. * There is no grievance process for this eviction notice; therefore appealing this decision is futile. The United Indigenous Nations expects full and prompt cooperation with this eviction notice.

* This does not apply to those persons who were stolen and brought to these lands against their will, sent to Japanese concentration camps, or have sought asylum here against other genocidal governments.

This flier was part of the Columbus Day protest organized by Anthony.

calling me Nigger-Nese (cross between Chinese and/or Japanese and African American) because I was dark and had double folds on my upper eyelids. It was obvious that I was very different from other students not including the other Indian students. I used to get called names often and would partake in physical altercations. I did not feel there was anything wrong with confronting bullies and standing up for others and myself. Authorities found this to be disturbing and continued to feed their theory of Indians as being socially inept. I was aware of my non-privilege. I was poor and an Indian, but I was not and never will be ashamed of it. I was and am still aware that people treat me differently.

I relocated and went to high school in an urban area. My friends were mostly minorities, but I did have some White friends. I lived in a lower middle class neighborhood and my friends were of the same class as me. I had to start my own club in high school for Indian Students. My favorite teachers were women who took an interest in my leadership abilities. They seemed to be concerned for my welfare as well. They were a stark contrast to the coaches I dealt with. I am a sort of a gifted athlete and began to demonstrate this ability at a very early age. Male coaches were never interested in me personally; they only wanted to fulfill their own need to become famous in the city for their coaching abilities.

The factors that I considered in going to college were very basic. It was vital for me to go to a school where I could study policies that have affected my people nationally and ensure that such policies do not happen again. Cal was a place where I could take those classes. However, my experience at Cal is one of isolation and a constant fight for equality and representation.

I took this class to represent my people. I know that there are very few of us here, and it is important to get ideas and issues in the open. I was hopeful that I could educate others about my culture, race, etc... I also wanted to learn more about the other groups. I feel that if I can reach a few other people, then in the future they can pass on the information. In a way, it acts exponentially. My first impressions of the other students were very mixed. But I have been taught not to judge by appearances and observe first by other's actions.

In general, it is frustrating to deal with White students in this class. I found myself getting angry. They don't perceive the world as the minority students do. If they want to, they have to change the way they think and that is difficult for them.

A time in the class that stayed with me was when I confronted a white female describing her "culture" as eating Sunday dinner with her family and having conversations around art. I asked, "Do you really consider that culture?" Her reply was one of tears, and she said she felt that I was negating her "culture." The other white students began defending her, too. I stood my ground to prove a point and the instructor asked, "How does it feel to have someone not recognize your definition of culture?" The room went silent. Sometimes you have to reverse the roles to get the point across.

Millie
Spring 1991

My name is Millie, and my parent's and grandparent's ethnic background is Native American/American Indian. We are proud members of the great Mvskoke Confederacy, which consisted of many local tribes (Southeast) and some that came from the Rocky Mountains. We were situated in Georgia, Alabama and Florida. As a matter of fact, my maternal Grandfather, Ahila/James Hill, came to Indian Territory (Oklahoma) on the dreadful and forced "Trail of Tears" in the 1840s. We were forced from our southeastern homelands of Georgia and Alabama to Oklahoma territory by the then President of the United States, Andrew Jackson. My Grandfather was believed to be at least 120 years of age when he passed in 1953. I feel very fortunate that I was able to know him and be around him for a very short time. When I was 15 years old, he passed to the next dimension. The last time I saw him, he told me I was going to be a great woman teacher and that I should always remember and be proud of who I am.

As a young child in the 1940s, my family was very close and the adults in the family spoke the Mvskoke language. My maternal grandfather participated in the traditional ways of our people. My father's side leaned more to the European version of religion. Our extended family consisted of my father and mother's families and we all helped each other with whatever needed to be done. We stayed in each other's homes like it was our home and shared with each other whatever we had.

Most of my life was spent around others of my own race. Way back in my subconscious, I knew I was different. I remember the love in my family, so when I was young, material things were not at the top of the list of things I desired. When I was sent to US Government boarding school, I realized my class was one of very little material wealth.

Others definitely perceived my people and me as different in the local small-town community where we shopped for goods. We were received by some as human beings, while others stared at us and did not know whether to fear us. I am sure however that they wondered what our life was like.

During high school, I lived in or near small towns, but I did not interact with the town people, because I only spent two months out of the year and two weeks during December in these places. I spent the rest of the year in Boarding schools without contact with my family. It is very sad to say that I did not really get to know my brothers because they were sent off to school in another location. When we get together now, it is hard to carry on a conversation but I do know that I love them because they are my brothers. This was all deliberate. I now realize the government was trying to break up Indian families and our land base. There were many such programs, all on the books, about the government's desire to breakup Indian country, which in turn related to Indian land. However, texts represented the government's actions as if they were for our own good!

The biggest factor that bothered me in coming to Cal was my age; I was 53 when I came to Cal. I thought all the young people would think, "What is this old Lady doing here?" I found out that some of the youngest ones held me in high regard and would choose to sit by me in class—which was very flattering. I chose Cal to come to for college because I remembered the 1960s and the Third World Strike; because I was here and liked what the students of color were doing. UC Berkeley has such an established impressive record as the best school in the world, that I figured it would be great to be here and I was familiar with the area. I was living back in Oklahoma and had just lost my husband when I decided to come to Cal. My interest lay in the fact that I have always wanted to portray Indians in film from our point of view—showing that we were not all savages and people to fear. My experience here at Cal was wonderful, and it created some of the memories that I cherish and will cherish for the rest of my life. My friends again were primarily the Native students. I really liked Helen of the Re-Entry Program; she encouraged me and all other students; she was very helpful.

The class was great because it gave me a tremendous opportunity to meet others in an intimate setting and dialogue about who I am and who others are—rich and poor and in between. My first impression of the class was "man, this is a lot of white folks to get down with." The fact is that most knew next to nothing about Native Americans. I remember Hillary, another native, and I took the class together, and we really had to do a lot of educating. Some people dreaded coming to class because we really played on people's consciences. People cried.

We exchanged lifestyles. We went to their sorority, and they ordered food from a vendor on East 14th St. or dined at Soul Brothers restaurant. We went to the bar at the Durant Hotel. We were snubbed at the hotel. I visited this sorority with one of the whiners of the class and had dinner with her sisters and listened to the meeting. When it was time to leave, it was pouring rain, but she ushered me out the door and did not even ask me to wait until maybe the rain stopped or even offer me a ride. It was like something she had to do for class and the heck with the human side of it—even after all our sensitizing. One pleasant memory I hold is that the class seemed to have touched a young man. His family donated the pool to Cal. He became very pleasant, and when I saw him on campus, he would call me by my name and always stop and talk to me.

Paul
Fall 1999

My mother is Ojibwe and Ottawa, from Ontario, Canada and Seault ("Soo") Sainte Marie, Michigan. My grandma is from Sugar Island, which is near the "Soo." She is Ojibwe or Chippewa, as they say up there. She is part Indian and White (Swedish or Finnish, I believe). My grandpa is from Sucker Creek, which is on Manitoulin Island in Ontario. His family name is Abotossaway; he took the name Aikens, which was my mother's maiden name, when he went to boarding school.

On my father's side, I am Mohawk, hailing from Kahnawake, Quebec, Canada. In the 30's and 40's, both sides of my family moved to Detroit, where I grew up, to look for work. All our family is still pretty much up there, except for those who left the reservation to find jobs in places like Detroit and New York City. My grandpa, ma's dad, was in the Navy in WWII, stationed and trained here in the Bay Area on Treasure Island. We all are working class people.

I would hardly see my dad; he would just work, then come home, eat, and sleep. Then on the days he was off from work, he would go out and drink and come back all liquored up, being loud and listening to records. Otherwise he was quiet. Maybe he was even in jail for a time or away staying who knows where. My ma would act as an intermediary between him and my brother and me, to protect us from his bad influence. Neither my brother nor I are like that; we are not rowdy or even really drink much at all. We both ended up doing well. My brother moved back to the reservation and he even got elected into the band council.

My extended family seems small, by Indian standards. For one thing, it's just my brother and me, and a lot of cousins. Actually, we do have a big family, but it's just that we were spread all over in cities here and there. We saw my cousins on the reservation in the summers, but we didn't really see much of the extended family on my ma's side.

I remember when I was probably around 8–10 years old, a young Black girl from the neighborhood was making fun of us, doing a kind of Indian war whoop. My neighbors (who are also Indian) and I were on their back porch listening to her. At first I was just shocked. I remember being mad, but she was a girl, so we could not kick her ass. Later on though, we still used to play with her.

I remember my dad would be drinking and saying stuff like "you're Indian, and don't forget it" and "you'll always be Indian." At the time, I was angry about his drinking and thought to myself, "Yeah I'm Indian, but who are you to be telling me like this?" Now I think that it was important to hear that, no matter what the circumstances are. There are many Indians who have no idea who they are or they feel shame towards their heritage. So even though I didn't know much, I knew who I was. My dad instilled that idea of identity in me by taking me home to the reservation every summer and spending time with the family there.

My neighborhood growing up was about 1/3 Mexican, 1/3 Black, and 1/3 White and other. We Indians were mixed in under "other," as usual. My friends were from all races when I was a little boy. I remember having different best friends—Rob and Mike, who were White, and Carl, who was Black, then Bongo, who was Mexican, and then Ronny and Jason, who were Indian. They were Seneca and Tuscarora. For a long time, those two were my best friends, and Jason still is today.

The one strong memory I have of Carl is sitting with him on my front porch and then seeing a guy get stabbed sitting in a car across the street. It was my friend Bongo's older brother, Jesse, who got stabbed, and his back was all covered in blood—it looked like a big tattoo. I also remember looking around the back of Carl's house for stray bullets and bullet casings.

Richard Martinez was nicknamed Bongo, and we used to hang a lot, playing like we were the Dukes of Hazard from TV. Bongo later became a famous drug dealer when we were in high school. He used to have a custom Jeep with "Richie Rich" painted on it and a booming stereo. He moved to the neighborhood where my high school was, and I use to see him on the way there. Then one day he was gone all of a sudden. I figure he ended up in jail or maybe even dead someplace.

Ron Pelletier's family moved in next door when I was about 10 years old. Ron and I were the same age, so we were well matched. His cousin Jason also started to come around too, and we formed our own crew with a couple other Indians called the Scouts. It was like being an old Indian scout—exploring things, being gutsy and making crazy missions. I had to be a good climber and fighter; I had to be sneaky and have physical prowess. We used to do a lot of exploring—abandoned houses and buildings, climbing on them and tearing down walls. It was like our playground since there weren't many other real playgrounds. The one good park was Clark Park, which was cool, but at night it became Crack Park so you had to leave.

One of the proudest things we would do is escape from the cops if they were chasing us. Since we were always climbing somewhere or breaking something we weren't supposed to, it seems like cop cars would always start coming around. I remember one time we were playing tag on top of a middle school and the police came. We were running through a muddy field with a cop car coming after us spinning its wheels, bouncing, and throwing up mud. I got away and was pretty proud. It was like leading a war party into an enemy camp and stealing their horses!

Later on, when I was in my second year of college, my best friend, Ron, got shot and killed. He had been getting deep into the gang scene and things started getting more dangerous. It was a lot of fun to be out rolling strong with your crew. It really was just an extension of the way we used to play when we were younger. On the other hand, I started to realize it wasn't too cool to be driving around all drunk with guns, and looking for people. The way it ended for him was terrible and I think a lot about how it could have been different if I was there when it happened. We had a lot of good times but I guess I'll have to wait until I die to meet up with him again.

Since I was little, I have been aware of my class. Our neighborhood was lower class. We were distrustful of people outside the neighborhood. We could tell who the outsiders were because of the way they dressed, or what kind of car they drove. We dressed nicely, but it was more ghetto style. We used to laugh at the "suburbanites" and throw rocks at their cars if they were passing through the hood. Later on, as a teen, it sucked because we didn't have a car or many nice things, and when I was hanging with others who do have those things, I sometimes felt cheap.

As an undergraduate at Michigan State University, I was 1.5 hours from home. That's one of the main reasons I went there. Detroit was mostly minority—straight up Chocolate City in fact. So it was a shock going to MSU because it was white bread America. It was cool though. I made friends of all kinds there. In MSU most of my friends were Indians or other minorities I met through activities with the Indian student groups, and White people who I lived with in my dorm.

The White people that I became friends with were a good bunch of folks. They were almost all middle or upper middle class, and that was a big difference for me. I met people who played tennis in high school, whose parents were MSU alumni and went boating! That is foreign country to Detroit! I was able to accept them and get along with them easily, even though they seemed very different from me at first glance. They also accepted me as well, but I could always tell they had strange views about Indians from their upbringings. I could sense suspicion from them whenever I went out with the other Indians doing some "Indian" event.

Besides Indians and Whites, I met a lot of other minorities while I was active with the native student groups. We used to chill with the Latino groups a lot, go on retreats, party with them, go to their dances, and they came to our functions as well. I met some down-ass people who were in it for the struggle: Blacks, Mexicans, Puerto Ricans, and a few Asians too. I had a Chicana girlfriend who was all in the activism scene. We marched on the state capitol a couple times.

I chose Cal grad school because it is a great school, and I had my sights set high. I also went to Cal because I felt that I had to leave after my mother passed away earlier that year; everything felt so stale and stagnant back home.

I took the class because I thought it would be good to get away from the straight engineering scientific people. My first sense of the other students was tension, as if everyone was thinking, will we really get to know each other, and what will they be like? Actually, part of me said I don't want to know any of these people! However, the friendships I made were the best things about the class. Some of the people are real dynamic and interesting. Tel was a well-spoken and educated Black man, undoubtedly a powerful person. He is a leader and can break it down when talking about the system. With his background, I can see him functioning inside and also outside the Black community. He knows both ways of thinking. Beto, a Chicano man, was also educated about the system. He knows why things are fucked up in this country and can outline the policies used to divide and conquer. Beto seems to be more emotional and more of a revolutionary. Daphne, a White woman, seemed brave and willing to help. In the class, Dave said "people who have made a difference are those who came from the bottom of the social structure/class and climbed up, or those from the top who reached down." She could be one of those latter people. One of the "assignments" she volunteered for was to help out at the American Indian Charter School. She came there for class homework but then kept on coming. The kids there liked her because she was easy-going—usually, the kids there are suspicious of new people, especially someone who looks like her.

I had to leave in the middle of the semester when my father got sick. He had a quadruple bypass, and I was gone for 2 weeks. While I was back home, I started to think about a lot of things that we talked about in class and how I grew up. I also thought about my dad's health problems in the context of class discussions and the history of Indians in the United States. I'm talking about the introduction of alcohol as a weapon to dominate us— about the bad diet and the diseases that came with it, and the whole reservation idea. It all leads to a bunch of lost Indians thrown into the city trying to get by—which comes from taking away our way of life. I felt angry because of all that and also because I couldn't really articulate any of it clearly.

I realized that it sucks to be poor. Thanks to friends, I borrowed money to fly back home, and they put me up. However, I didn't have a place to stay back home because our old house, where I grew up, was all burned up and broken into. I found some old letters and personal things in my room and other places—probably things that the crackheads could not sell or use for themselves.

After my dad went to the hospital, people knew the house was empty and went in and took whatever they could. Since that time, they also burned it too. That's the way it goes for an empty house in Detroit. My dad lost that house. He had put a mortgage on it to pay bills after my ma passed, but couldn't keep it up. When I went there to try and salvage things that weren't stolen, I found a notice on the door handle that the city was going to auction it.

I felt poor when I had to ride the bus to visit my dad at the hospital. It took about an hour and a half on 2 buses. This route was a hassle because I had to travel through rougher territory and watch my back. I didn't come all this way in my life just to get shot on the streets.

On the bus, it is all minorities; everybody seems irritated because it is inconvenient. The bus is always running late, run-down, and smelly—some people do not have shower access. When you come into Detroit from Dearborn, you see the buildings and streets get dirtier and more run-down. By the time you pass the stop to my house, the buildings are boarded up with graffiti on the wall with guys sitting on the sidewalk.

I could just feel all the little things adding up against me. I was thinking about all the institutionalized racism, policies that led to accumulation of all these subtle advantages of the dominant culture over us. They seem like little things, having to catch the bus, pay phones that do not work, finding a store open downtown after 6 p.m. All those little disadvantages add to a big difference—everyday everything you do is more difficult.

The people in power set it up good. It is easier to disregard those little things than it is to talk about big issues. They can just say, "get a job" or "lift yourself up by the bootstraps" to keep you from questioning why things are the way they are. They don't want to talk about slavery or government treaties. "All that is in the past," they say with a straight face. Instead, they direct your attention to a puddle at your feet, saying, "Look at that! What are we gonna do about that puddle?" and you're standing there staring into that puddle when there is an ocean behind you.

The bottom line is that if there were no White colonizers here, those problems of race and class would not exist for Indians. There would be other problems of our own, but nothing compared to this. The scary thing is that Whites would be doing this even if they were still in Europe…they would still be in search of people and things to exploit. Always needing something more, but what could be missing? We have stories about how the White man is the lost brother, stories that were told before we even met—so far it seems to be true.

Multi-Racial Americans

"I had my White friends and my Black friends… If I
wanted to go to a party and dance and listen to Hip-
Hop I would go with my Black friends. If I wanted to
go to a party and just sit around and talk and drink I
went with my White friends…rarely did these two
worlds mix…when they did, I often felt trapped, or
overwhelmed by who I should kick it with."
—Jonathan, Spring 1999

Ana
Spring 1997

My mother is the daughter of Italian immigrants. She grew up in the
rural community of Friant, California. Extended family was always
very important in her family and for much of her life she lived in
the same house with cousins, aunts, uncles and grandparents. The
only people of color in her childhood were the Mexican farm
workers that worked in adjacent ranches. Because family was so
important to my mother's family, it was devastating to my mother
when her family would not accept her relationship with my father.
My father is the son of African American professionals. My grandfather was a social worker, who later became the first Black president of the National Association of Social Workers. He is one of
the most influential people in my life (I ended up majoring in Social
Welfare at Cal). My grandmother was a schoolteacher.

My parents met and fell in love in college and later married
despite the protests of my mother's family. Many of our relatives

have not been in contact with my mother since, while others eventually accepted her relationship. (Ironically, my parent's marriage of 34 years has been the most stable relationship in the family!) My family is extremely close-knit and supportive. I am the third of four children. My siblings are my best friends and closest companions. I swim with my mother weekly; I play on the same basketball team with my father. Almost every Sunday our family gets together for dinner. I truly feel blessed to have such a wonderful family.

I was raised to be very conscience of racial and class inequality. My parents were both very politically active, and I remember sitting through political meetings or helping distribute campaign materials. Although, I was always aware and even proud of my race, I received a terrible blow upon entering Kindergarten. On the first day of school my father picked me up from school. A few of the White girls looked at my dad, and realized I was Black. They made fun of me and said they didn't want to be my friend. That day was a turning point for me. I can remember feeling sad and embarrassed to be Black. Later, when I relayed the experience to my parents, they sat me down and explained that some people were ignorant and cruel and that it was important to have self-pride and respect. In the third grade, I can recall vividly taking the CBTS test and having to fill in the bubble reserved for race. The question said to choose one answer. Confused as to how to answer the question, I raised my hand to ask the teacher what to do. My teacher kneeled down, looked at me in earnest and said, "Honey, in this country if you have any Black in you, you are considered Black. Go ahead and fill in the Black bubble." From that point on, when forced to conform to the socially constructed notions of race, I chose Black.

I was fortunate to escape some of the confusion and identity crisis assumed to afflict people of mixed racial descent. For the most part I felt lucky to be a bridge between two races, to be able to relate to almost anyone I came into contact with. Because of some of the animosity I held toward racists in my family and in the world, most of my close friends were Black or politically active and conscience people of other ethnicities. Looking back, I realize that I could have had a lot more White friends than I did if I had nourished friendships with White classmates. For the most part, I felt more comfortable with and connected to Black people, and this was reflected in my choice of friends. I have a surprisingly large number of friends with mixed racial backgrounds. In fact several of my dearest friends are Mixed Racial descent.

I have no clear answer for anyone regarding my race. Everyday I am asked, "What are you?" "What are you mixed with?" "Are you Puerto Rican?" or any other variation of the question of my racial background and identity. I usually reply, "my mother is Italian and my father is Black." I am then invariably asked, "Well, how do you identify?" I guess that question seems silly to me. My ambiguous looks should not imply an ambiguous identity, because of the one-drop rule in the United States and a personal allegiance to the Black cause, I am considered Black in this country. That is why it is a shock for me when I travel outside of this country where I am considered a slew of things depending on peoples conceptions of race.

I grew up in South Berkeley across the street from Oakland and on the block that was not predominantly White and upper class like the block above me, or predominantly Black and low income like the block below me. When my older siblings were younger, there were many children to play with in our neighborhood. Then, as housing costs skyrocketed, fewer children were around to play with. Unlike my brother and sisters, most of my good friends did not live in my neighborhood. I met them in school. My friends were always a diverse array of backgrounds. It wasn't until middle school that I consciously looked at the race of my friends. I was involved in athletics and political activism, so I pretty much spent time with everyone. The majority of my friends, and boyfriends though, remained Black.

I hate to think about high school sometimes. I truly look back and feel ashamed about how I handled myself. On the first day of school my freshman year, I ate lunch with a Chinese friend of mine. Many of my Black friends made fun of me and even threatened to not be friends with me. I didn't understand why high school was any different than middle school, where I would have just brought my Chinese friend along with me. Now all of a sudden it wasn't acceptable to even be friends with people who weren't the same race! I really struggled with this in high school. In fact, for this reason I made good friends with a lot of people but great friends with very few. The years following, my friends grew more and more Black and I wonder how much of that had to do with the social pressures I faced. I kept my lips sealed when movies like "Jungle Fever" came out and all of a sudden it was cool to yell out to interracial couples things like, "sellout," "jungle fever" or even "Uncle Tom." Now, it just wasn't cool for a Black man to be seen with anyone White, especially a girl, and it definitely wasn't cool to hang out with anyone who wasn't your own race. I can speak less for what was happening in the minds of White students at the time. I think some felt they were being discriminated against, but for the most part, the White groups were exclusively White because they wanted to be.

I decided to come to Cal for two reasons. One, I wanted to attend a racially diverse school where I could be involved in the community and use my opportunities to help others gain opportunities. Also, unfortunately, my parents had made it clear that the financing of college would be entirely up to me. Therefore, going to Cal meant I could keep my jobs and if I absolutely needed to, could live with my parents and save money.

At Cal I chose to major in Social Welfare, a very diverse major where I could take classes from many departments and still focus on my desire to bring about social change. All of my closest friends at Cal were students of color. I was involved in many student-of-color organizations, and I had the most in common with them musically, politically, and economically. I ended up taking the class at Stiles Hall because I had heard about it when I was mentoring with Stiles. I wanted to take the class to deal with some of the issues that haunted me since high school surrounding race, class and privilege. I took the class at a perfect time, for I had already learned some of the theoretical constructs of race and class. I can remember walking into the class the first day and noticed the stark differences in my classmates. I was very happy that there were Chicano/Latino students who were very politically active and outspoken in the class. I was also looking forward to learning and discussing the backgrounds and ideas of the other students in the class.

The class was disappointing at times, inspiring often, but always useful and important in gaining an understanding of race and class relations at Cal. Each week the class focused on a different theme, the experience of Blacks, Asians, Native Americans, Whites, Mixed Race, class differences and privilege. We talked about privilege in the context of defining each of our personal privileges. This was important because each of us realized a privilege that we may not have thought about. The year I took the course, there were two people with extremely opposite positions who often dominated some of our discussions. We took the class the year when proposition 209 was on the ballot. Everyone in the class had his/her own distinct view of affirmative action and the issue always came up at some point. The editor of the *Daily Californian* was in our class and when the *Daily Californian* endorsed Proposition 209, many of us in the class were extremely frustrated and hurt. It was painful to see that people's views on affirmative action fitted according to race. The anti-affirmative action side had set the dynamics of the debate and even the language that our class would use to argue over affirmative action was skewed.

Perhaps the most painful moment in the class came during our discussion of gender. As an activist for causes pertaining to people of color, I never focused on gender issues directly. In fact, at times I felt torn between causes. I never related any of my personal experiences as bounded by my gender. Then, in class we talked about things we take for granted such as the safety precautions we need to take as women when we go out at night, or the prevalence of spousal abuse and wage differentials. I became more aware of issues that will affect me as a woman.

I learned that the United States is even more racially and economically divided than I thought. I realized that many white people do not even have to think about race if they do not want to (and many of them don't). They can take for granted (if they chose) their ability to get jobs and have opportunity, and they don't relate this to opportunities for people of color. I think the class challenges White people to confront their privilege and make change in their life that reflect their new awareness. I have integrated many of the lessons I learned into my personal and even professional life. Some of my closest friends, including my boyfriend, I met while taking the class at Stiles Hall. Because it attracts student leaders, I would often meet people who had taken the class different semesters than I. It was always nice to reminisce about our experiences in the class.

Throughout the rest of my time at Cal, Stiles has been like a second home to me. After I graduated from Cal, I took a year off of school before returning for graduate school in public policy. During that year I directed a Mentorship Program at a women's organization and I co-facilitated the class. In the two short years since I had taken the class a lot had changed at Cal and the class reflected the change. The students seemed better off, less politically active and more concerned with making money than creating social change. I remember that during one class we asked everyone how much money they expected to make at the peak of their career. Only one person expected to make less than 100,000 dollars a year. During the year that I took the class, when asked the same question, many of the students said much more modest figures. I think this change can be attributed to the changing demographics of students at Cal. Students are getting richer and richer, and as a result of the ban of affirmative action, Whiter and Whiter.

I am now in my first year of my masters program in Public Policy. I hope to work towards changing public policy to reflect the needs of women and people of color. Being a part of Stiles Hall and the class has been a tremendous influence in my decision to pursue public policy. Although my life has been an open book on interracial relations, the class allowed me to think about and talk about some of the issues I had surrounding race, class and gender in society.

For new students, an education at UC Berkeley is a tremendous opportunity and responsibility. You will be challenged to stretch your mind in ways you never thought possible. Many of you will feel isolated and scared. If you are a student of color you may feel disenfranchised and outnumbered. If you are a White student from a predominately White area, you may be experiencing diversity for the first time. Soak it up, learn from it, and cherish it. UC Berkeley has so many avenues for you to grow as a person. Concentrate on school but realize that the majority of your learning will occur outside of the class. Get involved in community service; help others gain the opportunities that allowed you to make it this far. Balance your life with friends, family, community, school and service. If you play a sport, join a team, if you like art take a class, and if you want UC Berkeley to remain diverse, demand it.

Take a chance and meet people who seem different from you. Although you may feel more comfortable with people like you, it is just as important to learn how to cooperate with people who aren't like you. If you come from a privileged background, acknowledge it and understand how that will affect your experience at Cal. Put yourself in the shoes of some of your classmates who made it despite lack of opportunity.

If you are from an economically deprived background or a racial minority, understand that your feelings of isolation and frustration are normal. There will be times when you may want to give up but believe me, we need you there so much.

UC Berkeley brings back memories of joy and sorrow. Some of the greatest moments and achievements of my life occurred while I was an undergraduate at UC Berkeley. You will be exhausted at times. Some experiences will leave you emotionally drained. Take the bitter with the sweet and remember you belong here and you will make a difference.

Jonathan
Spring 1999

I am a product of an interracial marriage. My father is African American, and my mother is Scotch-Irish. My parents are middle class; my father is a drug and alcohol counselor for Kaiser Permanente and my mother is an elementary school secretary. An example of how my family interacts with one another is when my family travels back to Kentucky to visit my father's side of the family, the Black side. My father is totally at home with his brothers and sisters and mother, as well as family friends. He is more at ease, more relaxed. At the same time, my mother, who is White, is also very at home. I remember being a kid a thinking that my mother must have grown up where my father did because she was so comfortable there, and they were comfortable being there. If you were to hear their conversations, without seeing my mother, you would probably think she was just as much a part of the family and neighborhood as anyone else in the family. You would think she was Black. I use this example because it is these times when I feel closest to my family. I do love my mother's side of the family very much, however, when I visit my dad's side it feels like everyone, including my mom is so much at home.

My earliest memory of becoming aware of my race, was when I lived in Ohio with my mother's side of the family. I was in the first grade, and I lived there for about three months. The small town where my mother is from is nearly all White. My older brother and I attended school in the town. Now I don't remember anything specific. There isn't any memory of someone calling me a nigger or anything like that, nor was I necessarily harassed, but even as a six year old child, I remember the uncomfortable moments that occurred. Whether it was at school or out playing with the other kids, I just felt weird. I knew in some way that I was different, that my brother, my father and I were seen and treated differently. And that is when it clicked…to them (White people), I was different; I was Black. And as I got older, I was confused because I knew my mother was not different from them. She was White, but for whatever reason, I was not, even though she was my mom.

I grew up in a variety of places. My father was in the Air Force, so we moved a lot. However, I can say that living on an Air Force base, at least in my experience, was the same everywhere I went. I had the benefit of living, of growing up in a multiracial environment because of the nature of the Air Force. My friends were Black, White, Asian, or Chicano…I had it all. And more importantly for me, I grew up amongst a lot of mixed children as well. It wasn't until my father retired and we settled in Sacramento that this became an issue. I was sent to a private Catholic High School, which was predominately White. However, there were a good number of Asian, Chicano and African American students. So during the school day I interacted with pretty much everyone. However, my really good friends that I hung out with in the weekends were different. I had my White friends and my Black friends. And depending on the night and what I felt like doing, I went with one of the two groups. If I wanted to go to a party and dance and listen to Hip-Hop, I would go with my Black friends. If I wanted to go to a party and just sit around and talk and drink, I went with my White friends. However, rarely did these two worlds mix. And when they did, I often felt trapped, or overwhelmed by who I should kick it with. It was as if I had to choose with whom to identify.

I always knew I was going to college; it was just what was expected of me. My parents both went to school, and they instilled in me that it was necessary to be successful. I never thought I would get into Cal. When I did, I felt as if I should take advantage of this opportunity. When I visited the campus through the BRRC Black Senior Weekend, I felt the strong sense of community with the Black people that I was looking for in my life. When I got to Cal I stayed on the African American Theme Floor, which then led me to having predominantly Black friends as I do, today. I do have other friends who aren't Black. One of my best friends and roommates at Cal is White. However, on a daily basis, I immerse myself in the Black community. I feel very comfortable like that. When I go to a White Frat party for example, I just don't fit in, or whenever I am at a predominately White function, I just don't feel the same comfort level that I do when I am at a Black function. I don't limit myself to all things that are Black; I feel I am open to more. However, the Black community at Cal, as segmented as it is, is where I feel comfortable.

I took the class because I am interested in race relations, especially at Berkeley, which claims to be so diverse and liberal etc. I was also recommended to take the class by someone I look up to and respect very much. My first impression of the other students varied. I definitely had preconceptions of everyone. There was the White frat boy and sorority girl, the conservative Asian girl, and I saw the Black people and even the Chicano students as being on "my team"—they were going to have my back throughout the class. I remember towards the end of the semester when one of the White students wrote this poem that basically laid all of his prejudices about other races on the table. He was afraid of Black men; he thought all Asians were smart math majors, etc. It was the first time in the class that someone put that out there. It started a discussion that stayed with the class the rest of the way. It made me and others in the class think about our own prejudices and how we criticized his when I had some of the very same ones.

Another time, one of the White girls denied having any racial prejudices. One of the other Black males and I just couldn't believe her. We could not accept that she did not have any stereotypes in here mind about Black people, or Asians, or whatever. It was just so foreign to us. It made me really think why I couldn't believe that she was this way. And how on a daily basis I just believe that people have racial prejudices, whether they are aware of them or not. Through the class, I learned that through open and honest discussion, barriers could be broken. I also learned that I needed to step back and look at my own prejudices and stereotypes and see how I act on them. For if I learned anything, it is that I was not the open-minded accepting person that I thought I was, and I had things to work out. I am a U.S. History major with an emphasis in African American Culture, and I could definitely relate the themes and concepts that I have learned in my studies to the class. Mainly I learned that the social construction of race that we as a society have created is engrained so deep within us, that moving beyond it will take a lot of effort. But as Frederick Douglass said, "Without Struggle there is no Progress."

This fact came to me quite personally in the course of my final project, which was to interview my parents about their interracial marriage. This gave me the opportunity to learn about my family, which I am grateful for, even though there were definitely some things that I didn't want to hear nor could I believe. To know that my white grandfather, the man who I have loved and adored all of my twenty-two years, the man who I call Papa to this day, did not accept my father was something that I never expected to hear. It was the first time that I could relate all of the theories and examples of racism that I had learned to my own family. I am half-white, and I have always been aware of that. However, when it came to judging white people, or hearing about white racist acts, I never, never equated that with the white side of the family. For me, they were "special" white people. I had known and loved them all my life, and they loved me, so they couldn't be racist. Or so I made myself believe.

My grandfather on my mother's side never approved of my parents dating. Judging from what my mom has told me, he was quite infuriated at the idea that his daughter would date a black man. This is all considering the fact that they were dating in the late sixties in Kentucky—a fact that I still admire about both of my parents. Even when my parents got married, my grandfather, and consequently my grandmother, didn't come to the wedding. And for the first years of their marriage, even after my older brother and I were born, my grandfather refused to visit his only daughter's family. Because of his racial prejudice, he didn't see us. I was too young to remember when exactly my grandfather finally did visit my family. As far as I can remember, my grandfather has been one of the most loving men in my life. What my mother told me was that when he did finally come, and meet my dad, they hit it off immediately, like they had been friends for years. This fact made me admire both my father and grandfather. They had a huge amount of courage; my father for confronting and ultimately accepting a man who would not accept him and his family, and my grandfather for going beyond his racial pre-judgments and stereotypes.

I only have a few words of advice for new students. Be open-minded; try to unlearn all that you have been taught about race, ethnicity and gender. For here, it is a whole new ballgame. Be as diverse as possible, in all that you do: from your classes, to your friends, to where you live. There is diversity here; it's segregated, but there are so many different types of people here. Take advantage of that. Do not close yourself off to the unfamiliar. Take that as a challenge and get to know that unfamiliarity. For through that you will not only learn about others, but more importantly you will learn about yourself.

Woodrow
Fall 1996

My parents come from different backgrounds, one Asian and the other "White." I use the quotation marks because I don't truly consider my father to be of the "White" ethnicity. I believe the term is a socially constructed label used as a function of classification primarily in America; it is not an ethnicity, nor a nationality. My Father's blood is mostly European—a compilation of Irish and English, but with an Irish last name—and a portion of Native American—Cherokee, and some Shawnee ancestry. My Mother's family is mixed with Filipino and Hawaiian ancestry. My grandfather was a member of the First Filipino Regiment during World War II. My grandmother and grandfather met in Hawaii, where she lived, and he was stationed.

I would have to carefully say that both my parents were from unstable families. Both were third born, and both were the only of their siblings to have led a reasonably "normal" life with stability. Because of the instability of my aunts and uncles from both my parents, interaction between extended family was most always inconsistent. In this way, I think it may have had some influence on how my immediate family interacts. We as a family are really close. My relationship with my siblings is really close. There have always been people, friends, acquaintances, coworkers, etc., who have come to me and commented how rare it is for them to see siblings that are as close and open as we are. Not until we started hearing comments did we think anything of it, but now it is something I cherish. However, I think the strongest factor that really helped to mold our family's identity and the relationships between my siblings and parents comes from our socio-economic status.

When we were kids, our family seemed to always be in financial struggles. I remember one particular situation vividly. Sometimes we would have the power turned off. One winter when we had our electricity off, there was a very strong storm with, thunder, lightning, strong winds, and rain. How my family endured that night, as well as many other stiff situations, really helps to illustrate what type of family I came from. There wasn't a single argument between my parents nor us kids about how shitty the situation was, being that there was no energy, no gas to light the stoves, and hardly any food to eat.

In fact, quite the opposite occurred. We had an unforgettable bonding experience. We lit candles and began trying to save whatever refrigerated food we could by transporting it into ice chests. It was so cold in the house by this time so we all huddled under blankets into one of the back rooms, which had windows facing the back yard. We did not have blinds up so we could see outside at our big, dead oak tree that had all limbs but no leaves. Every so often a streak of lightning struck behind the tree, lighting up the sky behind it, illuminating what looked to be a monster. There we were, with no gas, no electricity, hungry, cold, but enjoying every minute of it.

I honestly did not really take much notice of my race until I came to Berkeley. In high school, my first two years were at a public school, where there was just about every race in the book. There were African Americans, "Whites," Russians, Asians (mostly Vietnamese and Chinese), Latinos, etc. There was not a real dominant presence of any one race. And I felt oblivious to the different racial cliques and groups for some reason. It seemed I had friends across the board, and I took notice of this and thought, "Hey, maybe its because I'm mixed," perhaps I never felt comfortable hanging out with just one racial category. So, maybe I was less subject to feeling the heartfelt issues associated with an "opposing" race. There seemed to be a lot of fights between groups of one racial group against another. I never fully understood why there was so much negative energy between two different ethnic groups.

Our neighborhood hasn't always been the safest. I wouldn't go so far as to call it a ghetto, but it is certainly classified as a low socio-economic area. In fact, when my older brother and sister were in the second and third grade, my mother and father pulled them from the public school system because they didn't like how they were being treated by the burnt out teachers that would constantly yell at them. My parents were sick of having my brother and sister defend themselves, not only against the other completely out-of-line students, but on a weekly basis against the unjustified wrath of the teachers. After some serious thought, my parents decided to assume the responsibility of educating their children themselves. I did not step foot into a formal educational institution and a classroom with other peers until I turned thirteen, when I enrolled as a freshman.

Through this process of home schooling we did need some sort of social interaction with other children. I think that is why our parents enrolled us into Tae Kwon Do lessons. There we met many people, and it became a major part of our life. Even through college, my older brother, sister and I have competed on the national level with the Cal Tae Kwon Do competitive team. And through Tae Kwon Do we gained a lot of knowledge such as how to respect others, and how to demand the same respect.

Jaren
Spring 1999

My parents both were born in Detroit. My mother is first generation Mexican-American. Her father was born in San Antonio and fought in a segregated unit in World War II. Her mother was from the Mexican State of Cohualia. My mom's upbringing was lower middle class. Neither of my grandparents had more than an elementary school education, but they worked, owned their house, and were able to provide for my mother and her four siblings.

My father is Jewish. Both his parents were born in the United States, but his grandparents were from various parts of Eastern

Europe. My dad was raised in North Detroit, which at the time was composed of working middle-class Jews.

When my father and mother first met, there were problems. My mother was the antithesis of everything my grandmother wanted in a daughter in law: Mexican, Catholic, from the wrong side of town. My father was the golden Jew in his neighborhood: good looking, popular, on his way to law school, and he fell in love with a poor, hippie, Mexican. The problem was based more on my mom not being Jewish, than her being Mexican. My grandfather remained indifferent and quiet, but my grandmother was loud and adamant in her disapproval. Ironically, my great-grandparents from both sides of my father's family, who were strict Orthodox Jews, welcomed my mom with open arms.

My father had no problems with my mother's background, but was neurotic about my future. Would my mom try to baptize me? Would I not know my Jewish culture? When my mom tried to choose a Spanish name as my first name, my father disapproved. I had to be named after someone who had passed away from his side of the family, customary in Jewish culture, which I was. Soon after I was born my parents split up.

Though I grew up knowing and loving my father, my mother was the predominant influence in my life. Consequently, most of my early experiences had more to do with gender inequalities than with race. Seeing my mother get physically and verbally abused, seeing her cry because of harassment, or not being taken seriously because she's "just another pretty face," are images that never fully left me. Because of her experiences, my relationships with women have always been stronger than those with men. I have best friends who are men, but I still remained guarded. With women, I am most honest and comfortable.

For the first fifteen years of my life my I lived in the San Fernando Valley. We had a house in an area with mixed neighbors and diverse schoolmates. My best friends were black, lower and middle class whites, Mexican, and some Indians and Filipinos. Our block was home to a family of white truckers, whose children became some of my best friends. These were men and women who had black and Mexican friends, but still spoke in blunt and racist language. These were also rednecks that intervened when my father was abusive to my mom. They may have spoken racist language and had racist thoughts, but when it came down to helping out a Mexican family, they did. They would take me along on their truck drives and I never felt unwanted. They were from the backwoods of Kentucky, and had a certain way of living and talking, yet still had a kinship with minorities, and watched out for their fellow person.

A big change came when my mom got married. I have known my stepfather since I was seven, so I had no problems with him. He is half-Jewish, half-Protestant, but does not really identify with either. When he and my mother got married, we moved from the middle class suburb of the San Fernando Valley, to one of the most affluent areas in all of Los Angeles: Pacific Palisades. My stepfather had lived there for 10 years. Our house was not huge, but I still felt weird living there. I didn't like telling people that I was from the Pacific Palisades; I would say West L.A., or Los Angeles. I hated living in an area identified as rich. When I would go back to Detroit (two months every year for 16 years) I felt quite different from my cousins. They all lived in houses; their parents all had jobs. Yet, I felt like I was the privileged one. I lived in sunny Los Angeles; they lived in one of the worst ghettoes in the country. I don't think people in California appreciate the luxury we have here. In Detroit you see burnt down houses, crack heads, and prostitutes by the dozen, and it has the look of an old city. Even in the worst parts of Los Angeles, there are at least some signs of newness or at least sun. My cousins envied me for this, which is ironic, because they were the ones with the tight family, the ones who lived near my grandparents, the ones whose parents were both married.

My high school experience was a trip. Though Pacific Palisades is predominantly white, the high school bused in students from all over the area; the school was a mix of all races. My best friends at school were either black men and women or Latinas. I felt the most comfortable around my black friends, like I didn't have to prove how "down" I was. I had friends from the Pacific Palisades, but there was always an air of artificiality about them. They lived in this superficial setting, in which Los Angeles was the only island in the world. In 10th grade, I went to parties where cocaine, alcohol, pot—you name it—were easily at my disposal. Eventually, I led two lives: my life at school with my black friends, and my life in the neighborhood with my white friends. Eventually, my two best friends would be a black guy from the hood, and a Jewish guy from the Pacific Palisades.

Any significant contact with Mexicans was missing from my social network. Because I had my cousins and my mother, I never felt whitewashed and have always identified as Mexican. However, I never had much in common with the Mexicans at my school. I don't speak Spanish, my family is from the 70% black city of Detroit, not L.A., and I am mixed. I would get grief from some Latinos for living in the Pacific Palisades, or hanging out with blacks, or wanting to be black. I think most of the Latinos at my school saw me as not white, but definitely not as Latino either. This is a definition that my mother and I have dealt with for a long time. My mom gets into arguments with people regarding Mexicans and their response is always "Well, that's not you, you're a different Mexican." Or, people will make a racist comment in front of my father, and correct him or herself by saying, "Oh, I know Jaren is different." It comes from both sides though. A Black woman tried to sell my family some magazines and went off on my mom, saying " I want a house like you got, ain't I entitled to that, I come from the street, lady." Both my mom and I went back off on her, telling her where we came from and explaining our situation. It's a no-win situation. From the dominant side, if you don't fit the stereotype, you are "different." From your own side, if you don't fit the stereotype, you're a "sell out."

When I went out with my first girlfriend, who was first generation Mexican, I started hanging around Mexicans more. Her younger brothers became my younger brothers. When her family came over, they did not give us any trips; I think they were proud to be in the home of an atypical Mexican family. One instance does stand out though. One day my girlfriend broke down and starting crying, saying she was not good enough for me, because she was so poor, and that I could do better. This was the first time that I definitely felt that I was part of the upper class. Here was my first love, crying because she saw money, houses, and education, not race, as the barrier between us.

The main factors I considered when coming to Cal were based on my mother's probing. My father just wanted me to be happy, and as long as I transferred (I spent three years at a J.C.), that was fine. My mom has always been the hard ass, making sure that I go to college and demanding that I go to the best college. Because she was the first one to go to college, and everyone gave her hell because of it, she would see me as a failure if I did not; it would be a slap in her face.

My junior college years gave me life lessons; Cal gave me education lessons. At junior college I was with an array of races, ages, class, etc., and everyone was pulling for me, including the professors. I also learned that college is a small part of my life— there is also family, work, health, etc. My junior college years remain my best memory of any college.

Coming to Berkeley from such a warm place as Santa Monica College was quite a change. To me, Berkeley is, and remains, a fake place. People of all races, front and change their identity, trying to reclaim whatever was missing in their high school years. I joined one Latino organization, and by my second semester became disillusioned. There were already cliques established within the group, and as a transfer student I felt somewhat removed. It was the first time, outside of my family, that I felt Mexican, yet I never felt connected with the group.

What was missing from my college life was a connection to a community. When I became a coordinator at Stiles Hall, I was involved with a number of Latino young men and women's lives, which gave me a sense of reality and bonding that was missing from my life at Cal. The coordinator position led me to the class. My first impression of the class was nothing remarkable. I had been in similar outreach programs and classes in high school, so I was used to mixed crowds. Our class was also one of the more mellow ones, where a lot of people talked about their backgrounds, but there were few conflicts until the end.

The most memorable moments came from three individuals. One was the Jewish girl Julia. She insisted that her family was progressive, that they had black friends, and that her parents are the welcome wagon for all races. I liked Julia, but I always found her story hard to believe, because my family has heard the same jive growing up. I still don't believe that if her parents' black friends were on an equal level as her parents, or were against something that was seen as a Jewish cause, that her reaction would be the same. I never asked her if her parents had black friends who held the same jobs or had the same income as them. I have been in many "excepting" white people's homes where their money and success have allowed them to have an air of congeniality. However, when those people are threatened, watch out. I don't mean to dismiss Julia's comments, and I believe there is some truth to them. However, my experiences with people in positions of power that say, "My family gets along with everybody," is that their gentle demeanor can drastically change when they are challenged. My mom has many Jewish friends, but when she made the comment at a PTA meeting as to why only Asian and Jewish kids were in the honor roll at my sister's school, the Jewish parents went berserk. "How dare you insinuate racism; your kids belong, but so do ours!" I don't know if Julia's family is the same; however, I found it odd that this so-called liberal girl lived in a very big sorority house with predominantly white girls, not to mention that most of her circle was white. In other words, it was safe for her to come across as totally open, when she surrounds herself with no one who would challenge her assessment.

One of the more opening moments of the class came around the second week. The homework was to exchange numbers and meet with someone outside your race for lunch or coffee. I met with Tiffany, a Southeast Asian who came here as a refugee. It was the first time I ever was in a one-on-one social setting with anyone of Asian descent. Our lunch conversation was laid back, but also deep. She was saying how she hates the way Asians around Cal act; the way they try either to act like hard asses or be total fakes. It was refreshing to hear her honesty and her resentment towards other Asians. She didn't seem angry, but seemed aware and real. Many of her gripes and complaints were the same ones that I shared. This was the first time that I had ever been around an Asian who had a working-class attitude, and who was honest. I think she later got upset with the class because she found it artificial and fake, and did not see where it was going. However her poem about her coming to America, and her overall attitude stuck with me after the semester was over.

The final opening experience that stayed with me was when Patrick, a White student, broke down and cried. Although his confession about his racism and fears were brave, I found it sickening and somewhat fake. On first impression, Patrick appeared to me as the typical nice white guy who wants to be liked by everybody. He was honest in his feelings about his parents, his black stepsister, etc. When he read his journal, some people saw it as brave. But for the majority of the people of color in the classroom, we saw it as "finally the truth, nothing new." I was not surprised by his comments; I was just angry. If he had come out from the beginning and stated these fears, we would have had the whole semester to talk and dig deeper into them. To wait until almost the last class, and to do it behind a "journal," is more safe and secure than brave and honest. Afterwards, I always felt a little uncomfortable around Patrick. I would say hello to him on campus, but I saw him as a phony.

After the class ended, I wish I had been more honest with my emotions. I never was totally comfortable during Latino week, because I was not like the other Latinos in the class. The other students in the mixed-race week were mixed black and white, and their parents stayed together, so I felt out of place there as well. For me to do a presentation in either group I would have to preface it with an explanation: "I am Mexican, but my father is Jewish and I know and have definite aspects of the Jewish culture in me." Or, "I am mixed, but because of the influence of my mom's family, and the pain the Jewish side has sometimes caused us, I identify more as Mexican." The class left me with more questions regarding myself than with answers regarding other races.

To any incoming student I only have one thing to say: put yourself on the line. Make an effort to go outside of your circle. Recognize that Berkeley is a lonely place that encourages elitism and separation. Challenge those notions. Whether it is mentoring, studying in a different neighborhood, or going to different events, you have to put yourself in situations in which you feel uncomfortable and uneasy. That uneasiness may never fully cease, and you definitely will have to make some sacrifices, but that is the only way to come out of this madhouse fulfilled.

My concerns regarding race and class have intensified now that I am out of school. Working at Stiles Hall keeps me associated with people from a variety of different backgrounds, an experience that makes my job fulfilling. However, I worry about my and my family's future. My little brother and sister are only 7 and 9, and have always been surrounded by relative wealth. My grandparents have passed away, and many of my cousins have moved from Detroit, so there is not a "home" for them to go to for the summer. Our house is big, our car is big, and my siblings have never had to see our mom get shut down from a job because she would not go out with her supervisor, or see her get physically and emotionally abused by a once neurotic ex-husband. I worry that their last name identifies them only as Jewish. It's not easy being raised a working class minority, and then to live like an upper middle class majority. To provide the best living and education for my siblings, my mother is faced with having to balance race and class issues, while providing her children with the best opportunities. Sometimes I feel that my mother has lost touch with her roots. She will make statements about other Mexicans, or make statements regarding class. However, I realize the drama she has encountered in her life and the years of frustration and pain she went through, and I know she deserves with the luxuries she has now.

I conclude with the story that best describes the dilemma we are in. My stepfather is the president of a Post Production company for movies and TV, and is a member of the Motion Picture Academy; thus, he has gone to the Academy Awards many times. One year in lieu of my stepfather, I escorted my mom to the awards show. I remember sitting there in our fancy get-up, and seeing my mom get teary eyed. She said, "You know, outside of Edward James Olmos, we are probably the only Chicanos in here." I nodded, and when we heard an award winner with a Spanish surname, we both got up and started hollering and cheering. We were the loudest people at the Dorothy Chandler that night, feeling a little awkward to be there, but knowing that we had to represent.

Class

"Upper and upper-middle class people see the world in terms of social Darwinism—'just pick yourself up by the bootstraps and stop complaining.' To them, my father didn't make it because he's lazy, shiftless, and worthless…the key is to help my people feel their power. That's what I'm dedicating my life to."

—Alberto, Fall 1999

Alberto

My grandparents and parents come from small pueblos in Zacatecas, Mexico. My grandparents lived off a few hectares, farming sugar cane. Zacatecas is one of the poorest states in Mexico. After the forests were cut down in the interest of corporate profits, the land dried up, the rivers dried out, and all the kids started to leave for Mexico City, Guadalajara, or the United States. Few can live there now.

My parents both came to the U.S. because there was no good work in Mexico. Both assumed they would be better off here, be able to make money, and send it home to help out. My mom came here legally and got a job flipping burgers at a fast food place called Mago's. Later, when my younger brother, sister and I were born, she cleaned houses, took care of other people's kids, and now stocks shelves at Target. She's been working at Target for about ten years with a promotion. Younger White people usually pass her up for manager positions, mostly because of her accent, even though she speaks English well.

127

Dad paid a coyote to come across illegally when he was twenty. He came here "Mojado" (Wet). He doesn't like to talk about the details. He has worked all his life as a day laborer, laying bricks, driveways or other masonry. One of his first jobs was as a gardener for two years, for an old White guy, whom he called his first "American friend." He treated my dad with respect and let him live in a room in his house. However, I think the relationship was rather paternalistic. Since then, my dad has worked six days a week, leaving home at 5:30 a.m. and returning around 5 or 6 p.m. He works on rich people's houses in the wealthier parts of Los Angeles.

They got their amnesty in the 80's, when the government made it easier for immigrants who had already established lives for themselves in the U.S. to become legal residents. It was easier for my mom and dad to become "legal" because they had kids born here, had been working for years, had a place to live and had never asked for public assistance. My dad is very proud of the fact that they never asked for any form of welfare. They studied a lot to take an exam to become legal residents. However, they are not citizens, meaning that they cannot vote. I grew up in a working class Mexican ghetto in West L.A., close to Marina del Rey. It was close to some housing projects where my cousins and uncles lived. Everyone was Mexican and lived in cramped three-room apartments. We had a small place, and I slept in the living room next to the couch and TV. When my little brother came along, we got bunk beds for the living room. We had uncles living with us all the time. Usually at least two of my dad's brothers lived with us in a room that my dad got permission to add on to the house himself. Sometimes they stayed in the garage, or at least slept there at night, because it would get too hot in there during the day. We all knew we were poor, but it was a good place to grow up. I knew everyone. There were plenty of kids to play with and the adults would hang out when they weren't working, and drink TECATE and play cards. There were some gangs in the area, but you kind of knew where not to go. Now it's all condos for rich White people.

When I was ten, we moved to Watts where we could afford to "buy" a house. Technically we own it, but the housing prices are still so depressed since the riots, and the mortgage was so steep that my dad will be dead before it's ever paid off. It was a shock moving to South Central. There were a lot more Blacks, and no Whites, except for the teachers. The teachers are often White people who commute from far away suburbs to teach in South Central. It seemed like the darker the place, the more depressed economically, socially, and psychologically. I could see it in people's eyes, and it scared me. I didn't know anyone and was scared to walk the streets. The first month in school, I had to fight almost everyday to prove myself. I would come home with black eyes and ripped clothes. You had to prove yourself to people. If you're called something, you have to fight or you get walked on. Once I made friends, they told me how to take care of myself— like don't wear blue here or red there, and don't say "Negro" around a Black person, even though it's Spanish for Black. There is often tension between the "Mexicans" (they called all Latinos "Mexicans" though many were often Honduran and especially Salvadonan) and the Blacks. The adults and the gangs were pretty segregated, but the kids mixed more easily. The Black and Latino gangs did not like each other; often you would hear of "wars" between them. Classes were sometimes crazy. One time the principal told all the teachers not to go out and to lock all the doors because the cops were chasing a bank robber through the school.

I was creative and had always wanted to be a filmmaker or an artist, so I became a graffiti writer. I was enthralled by the beauty of writing on the walls. I am not a violent person, so it was better than being in a gang—though I totally understand joining a gang—they're similar. They're both ways of expressing your anger and being with friends who understand what you deal with. From junior high mid-way through high school, it was my whole life. I always had my marker with me. You had to learn the ropes, to prove yourself. For some, that meant climbing a certain dangerous bridge or demonstrating how prolific you are or how much you could destroy. For me, it was more about taking the time to make the best style. Graffiti gave me a focus, a place to be disciplined, and a social circle. Yet, ultimately it was not a way out of the ghetto or a means to change the ghetto, but just a dead-end, so I gave it up.

Of my three closest friends, one was arrested, another over-dosed on speed, and the other disappeared to Mexico after doing a drive-by. I never saw any of them again. Partly as a result, I gave up drugs and started to read more to figure out the world and my place in it. One of the first books I read was the "Communist Manifesto." It made a lot of sense. It gave me a way to contextualize my life and experience and the world of South Central. I started taking AP classes and writing and illustrating for a local city news-paper. My parents worked too much to be around, and couldn't have prevented me from drugs and stuff. However, I think hav-ing a good family helped me a lot. At times in my life I have been very angry with my parents. I blamed them for making life hard on me. I used to worry as a kid that I had to take care of them because I spoke much better English than them. I would have to translate for them at teacher conferences, or for important letters or documents. I was really angry that we had to move to Watts. Once I began to understand the real causes of my family's place in the world, I began to become more accepting of them. I suppose it was a gut reaction to our poverty. I rebelled in Graffiti from them and from the world. Reading voraciously gave me the per-spective to understand all of this. It eventually also got me where I am today. I came to Cal because of its image as a hotbed of activism. I was shocked to find a big yuppie playground instead. There were so many rich kids. I was put off and disgusted. In one politics class, we were discussing the walkout in opposition to the Regent's decision to ban affirmative action. All these reactionary rich White kids who had no idea what was really out there were saying stuff about reverse discrimination and how White students were just better than Black and Latino students. I reacted passionately, as

I often do, and a few students told me that I made sense. I was happy they'd heard me and asked if they would participate in the walkout. They declined. I thought what's the point? They didn't really hear me; they just liked feeling sympathetic.

Most of my friends at Cal come from working class families. I don't have any rich friends. I don't have a lot in common with them. They'll talk about how hard it is to pay their bills when they are "broke" or worry about where they are going skiing for vacation. My closest friends are a first generation Pilipino whose Dad is a gardener, a third generation Mexican farm worker who works for the AFL-CIO. My best friend is half Mexican and half Jewish. Some of the Latino groups on campus put me off. Even though it's mostly working class Mexicans, they aren't conscious about social change. They mostly want to party. They tend to be groups that want to become assimilated. Their goal is to get a degree and a high paying job and take care of themselves and their family. In one sense, I totally understand this way of thinking. They come from Compton and South Central, like me, but what they want is tokenism rather than systematic change. The problems that keep my people down need to be eradicated. We need something creative to give the children a better chance—something to teach them why they are there, empower them, and give them a voice. I am dedicating my life to it as a teacher, an artist, or a poet. My goal is to find a cultural center in Watts.

My roommate, Hector, recommended me for the class. I took it hoping things would be exposed. At first, we were talking about irrelevant things, like cultural differences between Black and White styles of parenting. Then I visited the country club and home of this very rich White girl in the class. It was a huge revelation to me. At that moment I saw how she saw the world. I began to understand how people at the top are so surrounded by their own splendor and a riches they think that everything else seems hunky-dory. They don't ever have to go though what we deal with. That's why they don't change. Back in class, I told her passionately how I felt, and she and the other White girls cried. It was so cathartic to tell her honestly what I felt and hear an emotional reaction. It's different to imagine it than to see it. I knew few White people very well, and those I did know were nowhere near as rich as she was. So in this dialogue, I put it all together. White people, (and when I say White people, I also mean people in upper and upper-middle class positions) see the world in terms of social Darwinian. If we just work hard enough, we can all get where they are. We just have to pick ourselves up by the boot-straps and stop complaining. To them, my father didn't make it because he's lazy, shiftless and worthless. They really don't get it. I'm not closing off to the fact that there may be those who listen, read and really hear. Many won't be changed. I'm not totally nihil-istic. It's just that it's foolish to try to change most Whites' perspec-tives. I have to work with my own people. I have a real chance to do something there. The key is to help my people feel their power. That's what I'm dedicating my life to.

Preet
Spring 1999

I've been studying abroad in Scotland, and I don't need to stress that it's quite a homogenous population when compared to the Bay Area. Being of Indian descent has dropped me right in the middle of the largest minority group in the UK. You would be surprised what an advantage being part of an established minority can be. Everyone recognizes what ethnic group I belong to (no insistent questions), almost everyone appreciates Indian food (an integral part of ones culture), and most people respect our decision to be here. India was the jewel of the British Empires crown and that past colonial heritage seems to ease immigrant tensions now. No one asked the British to conquer India; they made the first contact so if we choose to continue the relationship on different terms... so be it. Granted, it's not that simple but it's surprising how many people have given me that rationale.

The point is only this—compared to America, I feel like I belong. The UK's social discourse of choice is class not race. Consequently, I am spared being cast into the lowest stratification categories. True, I'm a woman and of color but also true—I'm upper middle class. People here choose to respect that. They hold on to it and make character judgments; they perpetuate it by using various markers: education, accents, etc. Seeing the influence of class on this country has helped me realize the potency of social divides. The division of class is so deeply entrenched into the social fabric of this country that time has only the meekest effect on the power of history. It's clearly the case here, and it's very much the case in America. Only our national discourse is that of race, and our written history is not as long. My own personal experiences with race in America leave me as confused as ever.

I grew up within the confines of what I refer to as little India in Fresno, Ca. Little India isn't a neighborhood with tangible boundaries, but a transplanted community with strong connections to a medical school in Paitala, Punjab where all our fathers went to study. This transplanted community made sure my upbringing was quite strictly Punjabi. Though I went to a public elementary school and associated with other students of different races, my closest friends, until middle school, were just like me—second generation Punjabi girls with fathers who were doctors. This was always interesting to me, remnants of the outlawed caste system in India that still persisted. Though our religion was founded on principles of equality, the Sikh population in Fresno is divided along class lines. One side relies on the land to make a living, while the other relies more on family money and an education. My family invests in both worlds. My father maintains a connection to the land in the name of tradition. It is where we come from and what we do. Consequently, he is both a physician and a farmer. Most of the other doctors have dismissed this aspect of our culture and tend to regard the traditional farming community as a different caste of people, somehow less progressive and left behind. I grew up in the middle of this community divide. Each community has it's own church, it's own social functions, and it's own circle of gossip. My family is privy to both worlds, and this dual position highlighted the privilege of class before I knew there could be a privilege in race. While I was growing up, money bought me the illusion of security.

My awareness of race grew as I grew. By sixth grade I was very much aware of my skin color. I attended a predominantly White upper middle class elementary school. My community friends and I were amongst a handful of non-White children in the class-rooms. This made for interesting lunchtime questions such as: " Hey P, is your dad a doctor/taxi driver/or 7-11 owner?" These questions usually came from the pretty rich White boys who had nothing better to do. I hated them then, and I still resent them now. It's an unfortunate consequence of the socially scripted race legacy. I had my role and they had theirs. However, I didn't take it lying down. I always protested. I went to the principle in elemen-tary school. It has happened many times—my race being the focal point of ignorance and hatred.

Like the time I walked across the quad in high school during the flag salute. Our Mexican American security guard told me to go back to where I came from if I had no respect for our flag. Or the time I applied to go abroad, just last year. A Cal History pro-fessor interviewed me and suggested that I retype my application essay because of one typo. When I asked if I could just cross it out, she said, "I wouldn't. You want to let them know you speak good English because they'll look at your picture and assume you don't." I wanted to ask her why they would assume that but I couldn't—I was stuck in a role. I used to console myself that education could completely negate society's lessons on the race hierarchy, but I don't kid myself anymore. An education can be as superficial as one wants. You learn the lessons you want too and some lessons are never learned, except for one. The impact of race in America is a lesson no one escapes; you simply adapt to it. I adapted by aligning myself with allies on the race spectrum.

This race spectrum came to my attention in High School. After my experiences in the lily-white world I made a decision to be bussed to a predominantly minority magnet school at the edge of town. It's been one of my best decisions to date. At Edison High, I received two education's—one for the academic world and one for the real world. I became friends with women I admired: strong, assertive woman of color who said what they wanted when they wanted. It was amazing. My all-white, all-Indian world was suddenly influenced by the Cambodian, Mexican, Filipino, and African American cultures of my best friends. I felt empowered by the pride they had in their heritage. I realized that my race comes with a culture and that this culture is the greatest gift. I had what many fifth-sixth generation Americans had lost—a sense of identity beyond America. Prior to this realization I had stressed assimilation. I begged my mom to forego her native dress and at least try to be American. She used to tell me she could be American and still wear her clothing. I never understood that. I do now. My new understanding of America did not demand the complete denial of my mother culture.

I realize now that diversity is America's greatest strength. I help make America what it is; I don't take away from it in any way. This high school epiphany has held strong even today. I now understand my place in America but the consequence of this had been a rejection of those that still don't acknowledge my position. In other words, I've developed a rather disturbing negative view of certain segments of the White population. Namely, those I had the most contact with growing up—the rich White boys who turn into all-American Frat boys on Greek row. Not to mention their mothers who always used to talk extra slow around my mother even though she's an English literature major. That's probably the worst, the intangible but significant feeling of embarrassment one experiences while you see your parents reduced to "immigrants." The long-term effects of this are that I've mentally aligned myself on a spectrum with people of color occupying one side and white people the other. This simplistic worldview was soon challenged when I began my freshman year at Berkeley.

I didn't come to Berkeley with any false illusions about an active and compassionate student body, or a campus that remembered its past. I expected that Berkeley was much more conservative than its image suggested, and I was right. It is funny, I was cynical upon entering University and I'm more an idealist now. I always figured I would just get more cynical with age but it seems the opposite has occurred. Who knows, maybe there's something to this whole Berkeley thing after all. One thing for sure, I did not see it when I first got here.

My initial experiences at Cal were reeking of racial tensions. Prior to my arrival I had envisioned integrating myself into the same type of multi-ethnic group I had surrounded myself with in High School. I figured Berkeley is ethnic, right? Right, but it is hardly accessible ethnicity. I for one found myself lacking university housing and so decided to live in a home with thirty other freshman girls. Little did I realize that my new home was a pre-sorority pit stop and my nearest and dearest where now the type of girls I had escaped after elementary school. My housemates were predominantly White, almost all from Southern California, half were Jewish, and almost all were rich. Needless to say, it was not exactly the type of demographic I was used to. Luckily, humans are creatures of adaptation, and I found myself feeling more and more comfortable as the months passed. However, this feeling of security was intermittently lost when I was confronted with certain issues.

These girls were exactly the sorts of pretty types the society reveled in. Not only were they pretty, they were "White" pretty. They were the standard I was held up against and could never achieve. My constant contact with them brought out issues I never knew I had. The girls knew how to dress, talk, act, eat, etc. At least, at the time I thought they did. This insecurity in the way I had been raised, by immigrant parents who didn't teach me these "essentials," reinforced my old feelings of not belonging. The next year I resolved to live away from all of them and ended up cutting off almost all contact with the girls who unconsciously made me doubt myself.

I tried reaching out to other students of color but didn't succeed. The Indian kids had already dismissed me as a snob because I hadn't participated in their community my first year and all the other ethnic groups where tightly bound. It was a truth I had to swallow. Cal was not like my High School; it was like the real world. Different ethnic groups had to maintain a front against the white establishment but in doing so had to first preserve their own group's interests. Often times this pre-empted contact with other ethnic groups on a deeper than surface level. Beyond the classroom, my only other significant contact with a person of color was my sister. This all changed when I entered the class on race relations. A friend recommended the class to me after she overheard me bemoaning my lack of success crossing racial lines. I jumped at the chance. It seemed like the perfect opportunity to expose myself to the one arena Berkeley had failed me at. I was not disappointed.

I almost screamed with delight the first time I saw my fellow class members. I was instantly reminded of the classmates I had had in High School and the world I had lost contact with. It's strange walking into a world filled with people who understand the issues that come with being a minority on such an intimate level. I felt an immediate kinship with them. I realize in retrospect that living with all White girls in the appropriately called "White House" my freshman year had really affected me. I was able to contrast those feeling of displacement with the sensation of comfort and intimacy I felt with the students in the class. But I should stress it was solely the minority students I was interested in.

I had little interest in the White students except that I noticed they were in the minority, and I wondered what it felt like for

137

them. I imagined they were intimidated and I was glad. Sad but true. I had little sympathy for them and though I acknowledged the need for their presence I was slightly annoyed when I realized that the White students consisted of two frat types and a Jewish sorority girl. At the same time I experienced this sense of irritation I was rational enough to consider the lucky position I was in. I was going to ask white people point blank what they thought of other ethnic groups. This class was going to provide me with an opportunity to abandon the social script and talk to White people about what I felt and how they felt. Likewise, it was an opportunity to establish a bond with those who had experienced what I had to varying degrees. This was an essential element of the class. I needed to reaffirm my identity within the larger social whole, and the only way I knew how to do this was via an affirmation of my race. If my classmates of color accepted me then I knew I had not lost touch with who I was—a woman of color. This definition of my-self was reasserted and expanded by my experiences in the class.

It would be impossible to recount all my experiences in their entirety, and I hardly trust myself to do them justice if I were to. Therefore, it seems only wise to transmit the extent of my experiences by recounting the two main lessons I learned. First of all, it's not necessarily true that White Americans are incapable of understanding the experience of being a minority in the States. And second of all, issues of race are intrinsically tied to issues of class. Both of these lessons were learned during a mid-term section of class. The Jewish sorority girl had just made the statement that issues of race did not enter her life at all, and she did not notice the race of other people when meeting them. Or rather, it was never an issue. This statement seemed to me the epitome of ignorance and denial. How could she say that? I felt sure she was lying. In a society that built itself around issues of race, how could anyone escape the framework it had constructed? The answer came to me later in the session.

Each of our classes had themes and that day's theme was class. I remember answering the following question, "would you consider the economic class of a person when deciding to become their friend?" It seemed such a silly question to me. I proudly recounted how all my friends in High School had come from low-income backgrounds and it hadn't made a bit of difference to me. Then I went on to say how money made little difference to me, and I was very bad with it and that during my freshman year I had been thousands of dollars in debt. I don't remember the exact amount I quoted but I remember, an African American student looking at me with disbelief and saying, " do you realize that me and my mom lived for a year off the money you wasted in a couple months." He went on to recount his experiences in childhood and how he had not befriended some people because he knew he couldn't afford to do the things they wanted, like go to the movies or play video games. It was so surprising to me, and I had never thought of it because lack of money had never entered my realm of thought. I guess money is always an issue if you don't have it. Likewise, race is always an issue if you're at the stigmatized end. Within the social framework of class I had a lack of self-concept because I came out on top, though this didn't mean I failed to realize the issue once it was pointed out to me. Likewise, the Jewish girl benefited from the social framework on race but that didn't mean she couldn't understand my position. She just had a different vantagepoint.

The class was instrumental in my evolution beyond the simple Black-White racial paradigm, where "Black" included all non-Whites. I gained an understanding of a multitude of ethnic groups and realized the hidden diversity with each individual group. For example, my concept of Asian American was further destroyed as I saw that reality contradicted the myth of a unified Asian culture. Likewise, I was exposed to the tension between Hispanic and indigenous forces within Mexican culture. This education was a vital part of my understanding of race in America today. More than anything I realize that though race is an arbitrary social construct, it is relevant in the States today. It is as far-reaching as it has always been. The issues it involves span immigrant law, education, the corporate workplace, etc. For this reason I've decided to pursue a career in Law, though I've yet to decide whether to focus on immigrant law or Indian law. My gratitude to the students and teacher of my class cannot be under-emphasized. They've given me an understanding of race that few people take the time to establish, and this in turn, has given me a strong ideological foundation for my future career.

Gender

"I did not always feel as strongly as the other females in the class with regards to many of the gender issues they were bringing up... I found myself falling into the typical Asian female persona of being passive and shy. I hated it!!!"
—Sherilyn, Fall 1999

Just Once

Just once I'd like to
not shower for a whole week
until I smell like a man's sock
and grime streaks my skin
and people plug their noses
and say

"Is that a boy or a girl?"
as I strut past
shadowed by a cocky cloud of dust.

Just once I'd like to
go to dinner
and stuff myself with as much chips and salsa
and as many beers as my boyfriend
until my eyes are afire and my skin sweats onions
and my belly sticks out over the top of my jeans

and I am drunk like a man.

Just once I want to
tell my father and his pipe smoking mustache
to shut up
in a bellow echoing across the phone lines
Just once I need to say
listen to me!
Just because my voice is high
Just because I wear rose perfume and blow-dry my hair
        and laugh in all the right places
          and sit with my legs crossed
does not mean that I am empty.

Just once I will say
I am free
I am clashing shades of purple
and magenta streaks.
The energy of the world
Lies within the prison of a woman's curves.

Just once it will burst from my breast
and all will know
that I am life.

—*Joanna, Fall 1989*

Diana
Fall 2000

A woman comes in many different shapes, sizes and colors. At a very young age, I remember trying to be the best, strongest Xicana girl there was. I wanted to learn all the womanly things because the last thing I wanted to become was "Americanada"—(Americanized).

In my family, to be Americanized meant that you would be like one of those white women who didn't know how to cook, kept her house disorderly, and didn't take good care of her children—or at least not the way Mexican women did.

In addition to knowing how to sew, clean and cook, I also wanted to be strong the way my dad would tell my brother to be. I watched the way he instructed my brother not to cry, and I would hold in my tears. I climbed and got dirty with the boys—I was tough. But as I went from Chinese jump rope to chasing and being chased by boys, my body began to change and soon the boys were throwing pieces of paper into my shirt and grabbing my butt. But oh, how they would regret it once I caught them off guard—me with my big shirts, big pants and dark lipstick. Then they would give me respect; however, those games are not the same anymore. Now those stares could turn into something more dangerous; the whistling that once came from boys now comes from men, who can objectify me, erasing any characteristics that lie beneath my physical appearance.

Today the biggest challenge for me is the way I am perceived by men. I'm not denying that I like attention, but attention can come in many forms. It is one thing when a guy is attracted to you because of your physique, but it's another thing when he talks directly to your chest instead of you. I look at magazines and the portrayal of breasts and they make it seem as if women are special. But when I'm walking down the street and I hear "DAMN!," I don't feel like the models in the magazines.

I remember my first year at Berkeley; I lived in the dorms. For the most part, my interaction on the floor was minimal because I had already established my set of friends during Summer Bridge. In addition to this, there were other reasons why I kept my distance. Very early on, as I walked down my hall, I began to notice that the guys looked at me in a certain way. At times, my neighbor would stick his head out of his door when he saw me as if I was a woman in a fitness commercial exhibiting my body. This was nothing new to me, but it still angered me. Although they would be really nice to me, I could not ignore their stares.

Later, about a month into the semester, I was having dinner with one of my best friends when he casually told me, "I need to tell you something; you should be careful with what you wear." I automatically knew that the guys had said something and I asked him what they had said. I couldn't believe what he told me; in their conversations, I was not referred to by my name, instead my identity had become my chest. Why should I be restricted in what I wear just because there are people who don't know how to respect me? It wasn't like my breasts were hanging out of my shirt. They didn't even know who I was or what I did; they didn't know about my leadership skills. I was just an object to them. I was so angry that I kept my distance from them, hoping that later on, once they got to know me, they would be able to see past my physical appearance. However, this generalization that every cat-call comes with disrespect would be a misrepresentation and denial of my cultural experience.

As women, we should be wary of all men, not by hating or attacking them, but by watching out for ourselves. Being the strong woman no longer means holding in my tears; instead it means learning to identify what demeans me as a Xicana, a woman, and a person, and staying true to my culture. So when a Mexican man tries to catch my attention by calling me "guerita" (light skinned one), I am not quick to classify him.

I dislike how people use this particular action as a means to attribute many other "machista" characteristics to Mexican men that may or may not be true. It becomes a way of looking down on the Mexican man—who to them has become a pervert and a dog. But deep inside of me, I know that if a guy that I wanted attention from did that, I would not hesitate to smile. It just happens that this guy isn't the kind you like; instead, he has just crossed the border and he's wearing a hat, boots, fitted jeans and a silk shirt. When things like that happen to me, I am angry not only because it is directed towards me, but also because women experience these types of situations on a daily basis.

As an example, my mother would get harassed by men when she worked as a domestic worker. She also had to travel long distances late at night to get back home after working in the "fabrica" (maquiladora), risking her safety—just as the women at the New Mexico and U.S. border did before they were found raped and murdered in the desert.

Although women are women, we come in different shapes, sizes and colors and each of our oppressions are different—the fat lady because she's fat, the pretty one because she's pretty, and the brown one because she is brown. De la conquista a los Estados Unidos mis tatarabuelitas, abuelitas y madre han pagado gran precio para que yo heredara esta fuerza y no dejare que haya sido en vano. (From the Spanish conquest to the United States, my great grandmothers, grandmothers and mothers have paid a great price to pass on their strength, and I refuse to let their sacrifices be made in vain.) I refuse to believe that oppression comes in one color or must be understood in one particular way. We must let ourselves be united by our similarities, but recognize and support each other in our differences.

Katie
Fall 1999

As a woman, I finally began to understand the dejection minorities feel, striving to excel in a White culture. I imagined trying to prove myself at a business meeting surrounded by successful White men, feeling small, cautious, and unworthy. Most White men are unable to admit to the privileged position they are given by society. Such an admission would mean that a White man be willing to give up a free ticket to success and joining the battle against a system of discrimination, created by his White male predecessors.

When the women of the class addressed sexism, I was amazed by the conflict it created. Even the minority men who had taught me to look within myself to understand racism were defensive at my feminist testimony. This hurt and enraged me. Sexism is as deeply engrained in the system as racism is. The men, regardless of race, had trouble admitting sexism and argued that women have power in other ways and take advantage of it. But they argued it is a carefully circumscribed sexual power related to physical attractiveness.

I was a very active and alive child with unlimited dreams. I had all the confidence in the world, and felt it would lead me to bigger and better places. At age fourteen, on the cusp of womanhood, my life did a 180. For a few years, I had witnessed sexuality blossom in many girls around me. Unlike me, they received attention from boys. I began to question myself. My sunny, outgoing personality could only take me so far in adolescence. Soon my skinny legs and flat chest became the subject of mockery, and for the first time in my life, I felt inferior and unworthy. In my adolescent years during the summertime, I spent every day at the beach swimming and playing in the sand. I dreaded this time for I was teased for not wearing a bikini like my friends. When I finally found one that fit, I was teased for not being able to fill it out. The time that I had spent body surfing in the water was now spent lying out on the beach. Getting a tan and putting lemon juice in my hair for highlights became a priority as I followed my friends in their quest for an acceptable appearance, especially for the boys they were after. Of course such activity only made me lose myself more, but the comfort of fitting in was enough to sustain me for the time being.

Eventually all of my work to conform to the accepted standards of a teenage girl paid off. A boy two years older than me began to pursue me. From the start, I was passive and insecure with him. I did not understand why this boy, who could have chosen any other girl, would choose me. Nevertheless, I was extremely cautious around him for I did not want to mess up. This boy in particular had a reputation for being quite sexually experienced, and for a girl who had yet to kiss a boy, the pressure was on. I went into this relationship with the mindset that I was inferior. With my inexperience, I thought that no matter what he said or did was right, regardless of how it made me feel. This put him in the perfect position to manipulate me.

I felt like a sexual object that did anything at anytime my partner said. I performed no sexual act willingly; I was either pushed or forced to be sexual. I dreaded the point of every night that he would force himself on me. I had not a sexual feeling in my body, only fear and guilt as he forced my head up and down or yanked at my ponytail while giving him oral sex. I sat terrified in his car as we circled the neighborhood until I agreed to perform oral sex on him; then he would finally take me home.

Not only did the sexual experiences damage my self-worth, but I also began to feel ugly and fat with him. The derogatory comments he made about girls and their bodies made me wonder what he thought of me. He was very critical of fat on my stomach and my small breasts. He negatively commented every time I finished a large meal, and told me that girls should not eat hamburgers.

The one and only time that I stood up to him was regarding sexual intercourse. I refused to have sex with him. Toward the end of the relationship the subject came up every day. Finally he told me that unless I had sex with him, he saw no point in moving forward. I told him I didn't think it was possible.

The specifics of my early experience with sexuality may be unique, but I am certain that every girl experimenting with her sexuality has at one time felt helpless, violated, or without a voice in the face of a male. In my situation, I never said "NO." I didn't think I had the power to. I assumed that things didn't feel right because there was something wrong with me, not with the situation. I thought that since all the other girls were partaking in sex, it must be okay.

There is something clearly wrong with the messages sent to young women about how they are "supposed" to be—possibly because we are constantly measured up to women in the spotlight who are attractive and famous largely based upon their sex appeal. It is no coincidence that the occupations where women are by far the most successful include modeling, acting, and prostitution.

Common female stereotypes—passive, naive, nurturing, weak, emotional—are so strongly perpetuated by society that it is difficult to avoid being affected by them. Especially as a young woman, at loss of her identity in a whirlwind of how she "should be" against what she "wants to be." Between the two popular women's magazines, "Redbook" and "Cosmopolitan" the covers gain women's attention: "How to Get the Man You Want and Keep Him," "Quiz: Are you Jealous?," "Sexy Spring Lingerie," "How to Look Ten Pounds Thinner Without Doing A Thing." It is no coincidence that all the women's issues focus on sex, men, and appearance.

It is unfair to point a finger at the majority for the shortcomings that females face. Like racism, sexism is everyone's business. With so many areas of society perpetuating negative perceptions of women, everyone must acknowledge the detriment of the narrow female standard. Many argue that women are largely to blame and take advantage of their power in sexuality to get their way. In turn women express feelings of violation when reacted to in a way that they "ask for."

In class, there was a huge lack of compassion and willing-ness to understand how females feel objectified by men. The males claimed that if we don't like what is said then why do we wear what we do? They acted as if women set themselves up for male attention by wearing tight clothes, or low cut shirts. They felt that if we choose to wear revealing clothing, then we must expect or even want male attention. Whatever the female choice of style, it can't be assumed that attractive attire is an open invitation to take advantage of a woman in any way. There is much pressure and emphasis put upon women to appear attractive and stylish; it is part of our culture. It is unreasonable and inexcusable to assume that women wear clothes solely to appease men. Women should be able to wear whatever they want without being judged or violated.

The double standard at stake is that some women find that their only chance at power and acceptance in society is to use their sex appeal. Many women are successful at doing so, but judged at the same time. Although it is a ticket to success, these women are reinforcing the standards females should be steering away from. Society as a whole is guilty of accepting female appearance as an important factor in gaining success. Once again it is all a vicious cycle.

The only reason males are in the position of blame is be-cause they are the ones with the power to introduce change. De-spite that it is part of their sexuality to appreciate attractive women, there is a point when a line must be drawn. Although the feminist voice has worked hard for gradual change, many people maintain a huge bias against the feminist perspective. This is where it would be important for men to see the battle that women face with the accepted negative standards in society.

I have found that women have a love/hate relationship with their body due to the pressures they face. In a female sexuality class I took in 1998 at Cal, there was not a single woman in the class who could deny somehow being at war with her own body. This element made the class very emotionally charged and enlight-ening as women put their guard down to discuss their experiences of discouragement and violation. It takes much growth, strength, and positive reinforcement for a woman to feel wholly worthy and beautiful aside from how her body appears.

As a woman, I feel discouraged, saddened, and angry that so many women determine their self-worth, either positive or negative, based upon their body. The body should be cherished and appreciated as a sacred space—a beautiful and unique gift that we have been given to use throughout our lives. The female body is miraculous, phenomenal, and beautiful (although we get a different perspective from pop-culture where the body is made only an object of desire). I am literally counting the days to when I can truly believe this affirmation. I sometimes get glimpses of how wonderful my body is, but like many other women, I get lost in the quest of what really makes me happy, and what I think will make me happy based upon approval from others. A large part of me was lost in my adolescence. I have yet to find that part of myself when I exuded every ounce of self-worth and confidence that every human being deserves.

Sherilyn
Fall 1999

The first topic we tackled in the class was sexism against women. Not that I don't believe and support the feminist movement, but because I am a minority, gender comes secondary to my race. I did not always feel as strongly as the other females in the class with regards to a lot of the gender issues they were bringing up. Of course I hate it when guys whistle and look at my breasts, but because it seems as though my life revolved more around people calling me Chinamen, the words, "hey baby!," was a break from the familiar racial slurs. So, I found myself falling into the typical Asian female persona of being passive and shy. I hated it!!!

Abel
Spring 1995

The class opened me up to the fact that even though I am a brown man, I still have privileges because I am a man. There are things that we men take for granted such as walking home from the library or to our cars alone. Often women must plan out and figure out an alternative plan of getting around or just getting home. I also understand that because I have my health and use of all my extremities, I am also privileged when compared to those who don't have use of a leg or a hand, or who have been crippled by a childhood disease. This class has taught me to listen and sometimes even to speak for divergent opinions. It sounds pretty simple, but when someone says something racist about another group, then I should take the risk and speak out because the next thing I know, someone may be saying a racist slur towards people who look like me.

Power and Privilege

"I thought they were picking battles with the wrong person...I tried to defend myself and my life with ...my "educated" awareness... To my dismay, my ideas were shot down by some of the minority students. I realized that the pain and frustration that I felt for being judged as a privileged White female was nowhere near equivalent to the rage and disappointment minorities face every day in their struggle to stay afloat in our society."

—Katie, Fall 1999

Matt
Fall 1997

As I sit here in the comfort of a University café, I think of my brother—whose life is the antithesis of mine—sitting in a jail cell, being painfully reminded of experiences in his life that will forever imprison him. For most of my life, I've been searching for an explanation to my brother's profound hostility. After beginning my first draft I realized that something essential was missing. I had to begin over. This time with the most crucial element of my story added to it, my brother's darkness. I have begun to realize how his experiences have affected my own struggles with race.

I was born in San Juan, Puerto Rico to Susan Catherine Opava and Louis Kent Stitzer, both Professors at the University of Puerto Rico Medical Sciences Campus, both PhDs in Physiology, and both Caucasians born in the United States. My brother was born two years earlier. In fear of overburdening you with a mundane recollection of years, I will commence immediately with what brings me to write to you today, my story of race.

As I have said already, my story begins in relation to my brother, to the point that the first account I possess of race I've appropriated from him. When my brother was five, he was suspended from school for fighting. Some of my earliest memories of him involve his physical confrontations. Whether beating or being beat, I always remember his unwavering conviction to stand up for himself at the threat of racial defamations. *Gringo, Americanito,* even his name, Joshua, what he asked to be called in Spanish, was a death sentence by way of its simple pejoration into *chochua* and then *chocha,* a vulgar word for vagina. It was as if the attacks on him were attacks not only on himself, but also on his parents, his culture, and his entire race. His sense of pride and honor at age five was incredulous. He had no sense of being outnumbered. Had he known it was not only him against his 27 classmates, but that really it was him against all 3 million plus Puerto Ricans, he still wouldn't have cared. He would have fought to the death, all against him.

One time right off hand when my brother, father, and I were walking through the mall in Puerto Rico and, without provocation, a young Puerto Rican man put out his cigarette on my brother's arm. My brother was only 13. I can also tell you about the time my brother was expelled from Baldwin school for fighting with a ninth grader. Josh was 12. That was after he was expelled from Colegio Rosa Bell, again, for fighting.

I turned down my acceptance to Stanford University, stated by most pundits as the premiere University on the West Coast, in the category of any Ivy League school, in favor of the University of California, Berkeley. Turning down Stanford was an easier decision for me than most people could imagine. After essentially one day of my visit in Palo Alto, I knew that Stanford, although great academically, was not the place for me because of its homogeneity.

As a 17-year-old straight out of high school I was starving for the experiences that Berkeley would one day in fact offer me, in the way that the class so graciously did.

Although the class was something needed, I would not for a moment lead you to think that the class was not painful. There are several moments from the class that I will never forget. One that stands out was when we did not make it through the presentation by the African American members of our group. For some reason, their presentation, the opportunity for them to let the rest of us have an insight, however small, into what their experiences with race had been, shifted to a debate centered around perceived attacks against the White students. I remember explicitly the way Cottrell, a Black student, felt. Half infuriated and half dejected, he lost faith in us all. That day, even he, often the most optimistic member of our group, had thrown in the towel. Even during the time dedicated specifically to him and to the African Americans of our class, the focus once again, had shifted away from the experiences of African Americans and towards the feelings of Whites.

From the first day we met, students made it clear that they were going to take seriously their opportunity to speak openly and freely. One of the first things I heard from Chia's lips, for example, was that her life dream was to blow up the faces on Mount Rushmore. Chia, a Native American, didn't pull punches when it came to her distaste for Whites. To this day, I respect and care for her greatly, as is the case with most, if not all, of my colleagues in the class. I remember feeling strange during our introductions when all of the Whites in the group claimed some distant heritage to another race. All of us were hesitant to claim our White heritage. For me it was a peculiar struggle, because despite the experiences I recounted of my brother, when it comes to cultural identity I still consider myself, to a large degree, Puerto Rican. When it comes to sympathizing with racial struggles, I find that my own experiences are very similar to those of minorities in this country.

The screen of a far-removed ancestral tie to another race lasted only briefly. During one of the White student's introductions to the class, Nikki claimed some distant Mexican heritage on the side of her grandfather by which she considered herself partly a minority. Some members of the class questioned Nikki's claim. By all outward indications, Nikki was a privileged upper class White woman. She was the member of a top, overwhelmingly White sorority on campus, and her parents owned a house in one of the better neighborhoods of Los Angeles. Of all the people in the group, I know the class affected Nikki the most. She was affected so much, in fact, that her emotional distress carried over into physical malady and caused her to miss nearly two weeks of school. I'm not sure if anyone other than myself knows it, but the class disturbed Nikki so much that in the following semester she took a leave from school and attended Georgetown University for a semester. After that, I believe she went to Spain or London for study abroad. She eventually returned to Berkeley but I don't think she's ever really felt comfortable here since then. For the first time in her life, she was confronted with the fact that whether she actively discriminated or not, she could not deny that she was a privileged person in our society.

I will never deny that the fact that I am White makes it easier for me in our country. It removes the obstacles that were present when I lived in Puerto Rico.

Katie
Fall 1999

It has become important to my grandmother, especially as she grows older, to advise my sisters and me as we embark on adulthood and have to make crucial decisions. In any conversation she always finds a way to incorporate the importance of keeping good social standing.

Just the other day I was visiting my grandmother in the hospital after she had a hip replacement surgery. My cousin Drew recently ended a serious relationship with a woman named Lisa. The entire family met her at my other cousin's wedding, last September. As my grandma and I sat discussing the latest about Drew, I told her that I liked Lisa and that I hoped Drew could eventually meet someone else just as friendly. My grandmother interrupted and proclaimed that she never liked Lisa, and that Drew was wasting his time with her. I asked if my grandmother had ever spoken with Lisa and she exclaimed, "No, I did not want to and I did not have to. You can tell just by looking at her that she would not fit in with our family."

This launched my grandmother into a lecture about the importance of settling down with the "appropriate person." She began, "Now Katherine . . . there are certain levels of society with whom we just cannot mix." She explained that I was very fortunate to have wealthy ancestors of high social status and that mixing ourselves with someone in a different class was unacceptable to the family legacy. My grandma ended with, "I could not be happier that Drew has finally come to his senses and got rid of that girl." I never recall my grandmother even having the decency to call her by name.

Instances such as this highlight the importance of the Ethnic Studies class. Before, I would have excused my grandmother's message as senseless, exhibiting our generational differences. However, in essence, the words of my grandmother are representative of powerful truths deeply ingrained within American culture.

Growing up in Newport Beach, CA, I had minimal exposure to racial and socio-economic diversity. The people I associated with were White, middle to upper class Americans. The only minorities I had association with were the Asians and Middle-Easterners at school. Latinos, or "Mexicans" as we called them, are very common in Newport Beach but solely as gardeners, builders, and housekeepers. Despite this sheltered environment, I was fortunate to have very liberal parents who do not fit the mold of the stereotypical Newport Beach parents. They are not concerned with cars, clothes, or an extravagant home. However, within the context of my surroundings, I often believed that my family was poor, because we did not have the luxuries that my friends had. I often listened to my father come home from work, stressed about losing his job, and worried that we would have to move away from the beach.

While living in Newport Beach, I certainly saw the power that accompanied wealth, and I allowed material objects to play quite an important role in my life. I strove to achieve the lavish lives of those around me. It was not until I came to Cal that I was exposed to realistic varieties of people. And not until my last year at Cal did I realize exactly how sheltered my childhood had been. The worries I had about not being able to keep up with other families in Newport Beach are minor compared with what the majority of Americans deal with to survive in our extremely inequitable society.

The class taught me a new and deeper understanding of the word *privilege*. In America, privilege begins with race and the color of one's skin. The lighter one's skin, the wider the avenues to success. I was always aware that minorities faced obstacles in getting by in society. However, learning first hand of some of their experiences in this class painted a much clearer picture of how the American system works against them. The obstacles many minorities face lead to insufficient low wage jobs, living in poor neighborhoods, and attending poor schools. This seemingly endless cycle is perpetuated solely by their race. Some overcome their obstacles by chance and hard work. But they are still looked down upon because of the color of their skin. America is undeniably a White society. "Whiteness" is assumed throughout our culture politically, economically, and of course in the media. Everything is directed at a white audience.

White America often forgets the history of our country, one in which innocent people suffered so that white lifestyles could flourish. People of other races, especially Blacks and Native Americans, have suffered horrendous consequences as a result. We also forget that the Civil Rights Movement was less than fifty years ago. To assume that we have given back to minorities what we have taken from them is absurd. I have also realized that the demise of Affirmative Action has been devastating to this country. It proves that most White Americans are still solely concerned for themselves and have not recognized the severity of the suffering we have caused minorities. And yet, my most important lesson is that White America continues such practices of inequality today. All of us are guilty of perpetuating this dysfunction by going along with a system that works against minorities in thousands of ways.

In the class, I learned that I am not an exception because my parents are liberal and taught me not to judge. At first I felt attacked. I thought the students of color were picking battles with the wrong person because I am accepting toward everyone. I tried to defend myself with logical arguments, and expressed the desire to move on positively. To my dismay, these ideas were shot down by some of the minority students. I later realized that frustration I felt for being judged as a privileged White female was nowhere near equivalent to the rage and disappointment minorities face every day in their struggle to stay afloat in our society. Myself, or any other White person, will never know the extent of their pain, because we do not live with it daily.

It took me, who claimed to be so open and willing, about two months before I could put my defensiveness aside and learn the lesson of a lifetime. We are all guilty of perpetuating this system in so many ways. It doesn't matter that I came to disapprove of my sorority; I still desire its privileges. When I follow popular culture or watch TV, I perpetuate the system by supporting shows and networks, which most likely cater to Whites. By attending this University, I am supporting an institution that is against Affirmative Action. I'm not suggesting running from every part of society that perpetuates the system. I'm talking about giving back and fighting for what I believe in, even if it doesn't affect me directly.

Jidan
Spring 1996

One of the most enlightening experiences in the class was when students were assigned a partner and told to share their favorite piece of music. My partner was a wealthy Latina woman who lived in a sorority house. We met there to listen to our music and then had dinner. It was the first time I had ever been to a sorority house. Most all of the members were white and the maid was Latina. The cooks who served dinner were Asian. There were chandeliers, elaborate three-fork place settings, and silver candleholders. I could not believe the kind of college experience they were having! People of color were serving them, and they did not even have to do their own dishes! When I went to dinner, the sorority sisters were outgoing and nice. They commented about how pretty I was. Somehow, it felt kind of strange—do people often do that kind of thing? I went home and thought—"No wonder we don't agree! We live in different worlds!"

Afterword

A HISTORY OF STILES HALL TAKING THE LEAD

Those familiar with Stiles Hall's history have come to expect the agency to be both innovative and effectively aggressive in addressing issues relating to diversity. Founded in 1884, the early Stiles Hall provided outreach services to foreign students (in the days before the funding of International House) and generally worked at easing their adjustment to university student life. In the early part of this century, Stiles Hall staff and student leaders committed themselves to enhancing understanding and cooperation among Protestant, Catholic, and Jewish student groups on campus, and participated in the formation of multi-denominational interracial groups to achieve this purpose.

Stiles Hall's efforts to foster the establishment of a social order based on interracial justice and understanding did not stop at the campus boundaries. In the 1930's, the agency gave aid and comfort to several African American families who were harassed and threatened as they sought decent housing for themselves in Berkeley. Stiles Hall was also in the forefront of the successful efforts to eliminate the racially segregated admission practices governing general community use of the Berkeley High School swimming pool.

In the 1940's, Stiles Hall took an active role in opposing the dastardly internment of Japanese Americans. It organized visitations to the concentration camps after those American victims of racial prejudice and war hysteria were interned. When the war ended,

Stiles assisted in efforts at providing counseling and financial assistance to those who returned to Berkeley from the camps.

Through the fifties and sixties, Stiles continued to demonstrate its commitment to its interracial ideals. During this period, the agency played significant roles in bringing both Martin Luther King, Jr. and Malcolm X to Cal for speaking engagements. In 1958, John Martin left Cal's office of the President to become Stiles Hall's first African American Executive Director. In the mid-60's, the Interracial Retreat Program, under the able direction of staff member Bill Somerville, brought meaningful communication and understanding to an entirely new generation of Cal students who were struggling to meet the social challenges of that turbulent decade. This program touched literally hundreds of students, and many lifelong friendships resulted. The late 1960's witnessed the birth of the Educational Guidance Center, a Stiles Hall project, initially designed to encourage and facilitate the enrollment of low-income Chicano students at Cal. Today, the Guidance Center is the largest federally funded Talent Search program in the United States, focusing on assisting low-income high school students of all racial/ethnic backgrounds gain admittance to colleges and universities of their choice.

Stiles Hall has been particularly committed to placing low-income Black and Chicano students who come from similar backgrounds to the youth being mentored in leadership positions. At the same time, we have succeeded in involving students from a wide variety of backgrounds in all our programs. Out of the 350 volunteers, annually, ¼ are Black, ¼ are Latino, ¼ are Asian, and ¼ are White, with about half from low-income backgrounds.

Stiles Hall has been developing multicultural leadership for over a century. Senior District Judge Thelton Henderson (Northern Distict of California Federal Court), Former UC Regent's Chair Yori Wada, Co-Founder of the only independent Chicano/Latino student housing co-op Robert Apodaca, and Delancey Street (world renown Re-education Center for ex-convicts) Director

Mimi Silvert are examples of our diverse students, staff, and Board leadership.

Today, Stiles Hall is a trusted community center for many key student leaders on campus. Over the last fifteen years, over 500 have participated in our Interracial Relations seminar co-sponsored by the Ethnic Studies Department. Indeed, there is a large waiting list each semester, with participants selected from recommendations of current student leaders like four of the five most recent Associated Student Presidents, Student Recruitment and Retention Center Directors, Orientation Counselors, Resident Assistants, Fraternity and Sorority Presidents, and numerous other student group leaders. Still others have developed their leadership as Coordinators of Stiles Hall's intensive mentoring programs with inner-city youth. Bridges Multicultural Recruitment and Retention Center and the Incentive Award Scholars Program are housed in Stiles Hall. Finally, several Fraternities and Sororities have joined the "Stiles Pledge," committing regular volunteer participation and/or funding.

However, the climate for students of color at Cal is once again in the forefront. This is evidenced by: a decision by the editors of the Daily Californian campus newspaper to run the David Horowitz ad (not article) which argues against reparations against slavery; the decision by Bridges Multicultural Recruitment and Retention Center to withdraw their support for the University's outreach efforts and this decision's impact on financial support from the University; the recent "Black Out," where black students, supported primarily by Latino students, dressed in all black, wore bandanas across their mouths, silently attended their classes, passed out informational fliers describing either being attacked or ignored, and blocked Sather Gate, evoking images of power and solidarity, much like the Civil Rights struggle of the 1960's.

Appendix A

COURSE SYLLABUS

Purpose:

To provide student leaders from diverse racial, ethnic, and class backgrounds the opportunity to learn from and with each other about issues of racial, class and gender conflict and common ground in an atmosphere of openness and mutual engagement and respect.

Requirements:

1. Consistent participation. *Attend all sessions*
2. Arrive on time and participate fully.
3. Lead one session with fellow students around your own racial/class/gender identity.
4. A creative, experiential project related to race, class or gender.
5. Weekly selections from reader and four homework assignments from your peers.
6. Weekly journal entries recording thoughts and feelings.

The following are some examples of activities and homework assignments, which students report back at the next class while sharing their feelings and insights and discussing others' reactions. This syllabus is an evolving guide for interested staff or faculty. Student engagement and accompanying homework and activities are at the center of the curriculum. Theoretical concepts and scholarly research on the issues of race, gender, and class become a part of the curriculum when students introduce them from other University courses.

Week 1 & 2 **Introductions, Overview, and Expectations**

Activity: Students share: a funny story or painful lesson, a typical family interaction, their first experience of recognizing their "difference," high school and college clique to which they belong, hopes and fears, and what lifts them up when they're down.

Homework: Interracial pairs share a favorite piece of music and discuss. In the second week, a different pair shares a favorite piece of poetry or prose.

Reading: "Race, Gender, and Class" Shaef; "Stigma & Social Identity" Goff.

Week 3 **Gender**

Activity: Men are blindfolded, on their knees in the dark while women read sexual assault statistics. Men are rated by women in a beauty contest with catcalls. In men and women's groups, they discuss what they like and dislike about men and women.

Homework: Men can only go out after dark with a formal escort, wear "I have a small penis" T-shirt, or wear menstrual pads for a day.

Reading: "Phenomenal Woman" Angelou; "The Chalice & the Blade" McReynolds.

Week 4 **Chicano/Latino**

Activity: Role-play a third grade class speaking only Spanish. Role-play "Driving while Brown."

Homework: Participate in "El Grito" celebration, attend a Spanish-speaking Mass, or spend time with day laborers.

Reading: "The Educated One" Guerrero; "Por El Amor de Mi Madre" Pallan; "At the Slaughterhouse" New York Times.

Week 5 **Asian American**

Activity: Brainstorm Asian stereotypes and discuss. Role-play what it would feel like to enter a mostly Asian pre-med class.
Homework: Tutor inner-city Asian youth, or attend an Asian student group meeting.
Reading: "Why I get Angry" Boquiren; "On the Wrong Side" Chang; "Mandate of Heaven" Sze.

Week 6 **African American**

Activity: Silently view displayed statistics affecting the Black community. Discuss racism's impact then put a dollar value on how much it would take to be black in America, and note discrepancies.
Homework: Attend a classmate's Gospel Church Service, attend a Black Recruitment & Retention Meeting, or see "Ethnic Notions."
Reading: "Rage of the Privileged Class" Close; "Street Soldiers" Marshall; "Standing Out at Work" New York Times.

Week 7 **European American**

Activity: List stereotypes of whites on board and discuss. Write down "Why do Whites…?" and get responses.
Homework: Attend a Sorority Dinner, attend rugby or tennis match, or go to a classmate's country club.
Reading: "Quiet Rage" Rubin; "Crossings" Harrington; "Plea for the Dead" Wiesel

*Week 8 **Native American**

Activity: Cluster in small, crowded areas and get moved arbitrarily. Learn about the reality vs. myth of Indians. Discuss Bureau of Indian Affairs historical roles.
Homework: Attend a pow-wow, or tutor urban or reservation Indian students.

---

*Native American and Mixed Racial Descent students generally represent a smaller proportion of the students in the class and are addressed in one week.

Reading: "Cultural Comparisons" Red Voices; "Chief Seattle's Address."

Mixed Racial Descent

Activity: Discuss interracial dating, marriage, and children

Homework: Attend a class or support group for people of mixed-racial descent, i.e. Happa Issues Forum.

Reading: "The Multi-Racial Experience" Root; "The Color of Water" McBride.

Week 9 Class Issues in the U.S.

Activity: Make an anonymous chart of each student's family's net wealth and discuss, noting the wide range.

Homework: Spend five dollars on all needs for three days, apply for food stamps or financial aid, or live without computer and cell phone for three days.

Reading: "Wealth Addiction" Slater; "Redneck Manifesto" Goad.

Week 10 Power and Privilege

Activity: Identify areas of personal privilege like not being homeless or hungry, not being exposed to drug addiction, or will graduate from an elite University.

Homework: Hold hands with a classmate of the same gender on campus.

Reading: "White Privilege" McIntosh; "Institutional Racism" Seldon; "The Needs of Gay and Lesbian Teenagers" Smith.

Week 11-13 Final Projects

Share what you learned in taking on a personal challenge regarding race, class, and gender (i.e. interview a grandparent about their past, write a poem, or confront a friend or relative about their views).

Reading: "Race Matters" West.

Week 14 **Summary and Course Evaluation**

Share joy and frustrations about class. Tell someone what you appreciate about them and what you learned from them. Bring a potluck dish to share.
Reading: "Fire Next Time" Baldwin.

Appendix B

FRESHMEN ENROLLED AT U.C. BERKELEY

	African American	Chicano Latino	Native American
1987	447	602	74
	12.3%	16.6%	2%
1997	257	472	23
	7.2%	13.2%	0.6%
1998	126	271	14
	3.4%	7.3%	0.3%
2000	148	329	20
	4%	8.8%	0.5%

	Asian American	European American	Other, No Data and International
1987	881	1398	231
	24%	38%	6%
1997	1468	1018	335
	41%	28.5%	9%
1998	1565	1090	669
	41.9%	29.2%	17.9%
2000	1634	1124	481
	43.7%	30%	12.9%

Office of Student Research, U.C. Berkeley

The course was first fully implemented in 1987. The student body was substantially diverse. As a result of SP 1 and 2 (U.C. Regent's ban on affirmative action in admissions and faculty hiring) and Proposition 209 (statewide ban on affirmative action in admissions, hiring and contracting), the numbers of underrepresented minorities at U.C. Berkeley decreased precipitously. For many students, the social isolation and elitism is now more prevalent. These factors make the need for a seminar like this, where underrepresented minorities are in the majority, more crucial than ever.